THE DYADIC
TRANSACTION

THE DYADIC TRANSACTION

An Investigation into the Nature
of the Psychotherapeutic Process

Samuel Eisenstein
Norman A. Levy
& Judd Marmor

Transaction Publishers
New Brunswick (U.S.A.) and London (U.K.)

Library of Congress Catalog Number: 93-23866
ISBN: 1-56000-136-4
Printed in the United States of America

Library of Congress Cataloging-in-Publication Data

Eisenstein, Samuel, 1913–
    The dyadic transaction : an investigation into the nature of the
psychotherapeutic process / Samuel Eisenstein, Norman A. Levy, Judd
Marmor.
        p.   cm.
    Includes bibliographical references and index.
    ISBN 1-56000-136-4
    1. Psychotherapist and patient—Case studies.   2. Psychotherapy—
Case studies.   I. Levy, Norman A., 1907–   .   II. Marmor, Judd, 1910–   .
III. Title.
RC480.8.E37   1993
616.89′14—dc20   93-23866
                                                                          CIP

*This book is dedicated
to the memory of Franz Alexander*

Contents

Preface

The research on which this book is based was begun late in 1956 and completed in 1960, although the processing of the data then continued for many more months. Why then has it taken so long to bring it to publication?

The major cause was the unexpected and untimely death in 1961 of Franz Alexander to whom this book is dedicated. Alexander was the initiator, therapist, and primary investigator of the project and devoted a substantial amount of his time to its direction and administration. With his passing, the arduous processing of the voluminous data that we were in the midst of at that time, came to a halt.

The authors of this volume, however, were unable to let the matter rest. We never lost our awareness of the historical importance of this project and of the scientific value of the material. After a number of years, therefore, we were able to resume the processing of the data with which we had been directly involved as observers, and brought the volume to its present conclusion.

We are cognizant of the fact, of course, that in the long interim other researchers on the nature of the psychotherapeutic process have published their findings (see Review of Literature). To the best of our knowledge, however, the painstaking analysis, hour by hour, of a long-term psychoanalytically oriented psychotherapy, based on the carefully organized, independent observations of several experienced psychoanalysts, which is represented by the present work, has not been duplicated elsewhere. The comparison of the therapist's impression of what was going on in the sessions with those of the outside observers is another unique feature of the present work that is of special interest.

Thus, although the impact that this volume might have had had it appeared in the early 1960s has been softened by the passage of time, we believe it still to be a contribution of major importance to the elucidation of the complex process of psychoanalytically oriented psychotherapy within a dyadic framework.

The authors wish to thank Mrs. Lena Pincus and Mrs. Phyllis Goldman for their efficient work in preparing this manuscript for publication.

1

History of the Project

Traditionally the study of the psychotherapeutic process was based on the observation of the therapist him or herself. The mid-twentieth-century surge of research in the psychotherapeutic process was the consequence of the realization of the inadequacy of these traditional methods.

Prior to 1950 hardly any significant study of the psychoanalytic transaction was available. All of the major attempts at a systematic scientific investigation of the psychotherapeutic process took place after that date. In addition to innumerable small projects carried out by one or two individual investigators, in relatively limited areas of psychotherapy, there were several major multidisciplinary group projects, such as the Phipps Psychotherapy Research Project and the Illinois Neuropsychiatric Institute Project under the direction of Dr. David Shakow, who later moved to Bethesda and continued the project there. Two of the earliest, though not interdisciplinary, were the University of Chicago's Counseling Center Research on Client-Centered Therapy, and the series of research studies that originated at the University of Michigan. The first National Institute of Mental Health (NIMH)-sponsored Conference on Research in Psychotherapy took place in 1958, followed by the second conference in 1961.

In 1957 a group of researchers under the direction of Dr. Franz Alexander, director of the Psychiatric and Psychosomatic Research Institute of Mount Sinai Hospital in Los Angeles, with a grant from

1

the Ford Foundation, initiated a systematic scientific study of the psychotherapeutic process. Dr. Alexander, as principal investigator, organized a research group consisting of nine accredited psychoanalysts, one psychoanalytically trained clinical psychologist, and a social psychologist.

In the original proposal for the Study of the Psychotherapeutic Process, Alexander stated that the purpose of the study was to describe and understand more precisely and in detail the psychological processes that occur during psychoanalysis and psychoanalytically oriented psychotherapy. More specifically, the goal was to evaluate the changes in the patient's personality that may result from such treatment, and to account step by step for the development of such changes. Alexander's principal motivation for undertaking this study was his observation that most of our knowledge of the psychoanalytic therapy and psychotherapeutic process came from incompletely recorded or recalled material, usually based on the therapist's own evaluation of what transpired during the therapeutic relationship. The therapist's reconstructions were not checked against observations and interpretations of others who were not involved in the therapeutic process. Another gap in our knowledge concerning psychoanalytic therapy arose from the lack of systematic information concerning the therapist's conscious reasons for his or her interpretations. Finally, Alexander pointed out that too little was known about the influence of the analyst's personality on his or her therapeutic behavior. The relevance of the therapist's idiosyncratic qualities, values, residual neurosis, and past and current life experiences had been recognized but never systematically studied.

Psychotherapy research in the mid-1950s was conceptualized in dichotomies: outcome versus process; experimental design versus naturalistic observation; psychoanalytic versus nonanalytic theoretical orientation. The Ford Foundation Project, as this research was known, was clearly conceived as a process study of psychoanalytic therapy. The methodology was to be primarily the case study approach, relying on carefully controlled naturalistic observation as the basic research tool.

The aim of the proposed research was to collect basic information concerning the therapeutic process in a systematic fashion through the intensive study of a relatively small number of cases. It was hoped that the investigation would permit the tentative formulation and testing of some hypotheses. The specific foci of interest for the study were to be (a) the role of the therapist in the therapeutic process; (b) the effects of psychoanalytic therapy on the patient and investigation of the factors that may account for changes; and (c) a comparison between the process of cases in psychoanalysis and in psychoanalytic psychotherapy.

Although the members of the research team shared the basic theoretical framework of psychoanalysis, they had no common tradition of research methodology. Therefore the group needed a period of working together as a team in order to clarify their thoughts about the definition of significant data, agree upon a reasonably clear and shared language, and, particularly, to decide on standardized means of observing and recording. Before any data were collected, the research team met for regular weekly planning conferences from December 1956 to January 1958, when the actual project was begun.

In the course of the planning conferences, the members of the group very soon became aware that because of the limitations of time and budget, certain choices had to be made. If the emphasis was to be on a comparison between traditional psychoanalytic technique and psychoanalytic psychotherapy, then a larger number of cases had to be studied, permitting the observation of a variety of therapists using different techniques. If, on the other hand, the emphasis was to be on the therapeutic process per se, that is, on the sequential relationship between patient-therapist interactions and intrapsychic as well as behavioral changes in the patient, then an intensive hour-by-hour, perhaps minute-by-minute study was indicated; and this could only be undertaken for a very small sample. After much deliberation, the group finally decided to study one patient treated with the psychoanalytic technique and another with psychoanalytic psychotherapy. The two forms of therapy were to be differentiated by the number of weekly hours; by the position on the couch versus sitting up in the chair; and by the presence or absence of a consistent, explicit enforcement of the fundamental rule. Patients were to be selected on the basis of specified criteria to ensure their suitability for the form of therapy selected for them, including their ability to meet the requirements of the project, that is, completion of therapy, frequency and time of hours, and, especially, their willingness to accept the condition of being observed.

Originally, diagnostic psychological tests and extensive social case work data were to be included in the information used for selecting patients. However, the group felt that the therapist should be free to follow his usual office routine. It was argued that since this was a naturalistic study of the psychoanalytic or psychotherapeutic process, the therapist should not be required to rely on psychological tests and/or social history data as a basis for accepting a patient for therapy if this was not his usual procedure. As long as the goal was to study the process as it "really is," it was argued that the fewer artifacts introduced and the less the therapist was "fenced in," the better. Furthermore, everybody on the team agreed that it was at best a very difficult task to conduct a therapy while being observed by one's colleagues, and that therefore whatever could be done to make the therapist comfortable and allow him to work in his accustomed manner would eventually result in a better study.

After several months of group discussions it was decided that observation techniques and recording methods could best be developed in the process of actually observing live patient-therapist interactions. Also, it was felt that the therapists who were going to conduct the observed analyses or therapies needed some experience in being observed before they actually embarked on the project proper. It is difficult to realize today, twenty-five years later, that with one or two exceptions, none of the members of the research team had ever observed another therapist or been themselves observed in action. It is impossible to describe the feeling of adventure and risk with which all therapists and observers approached the actual start of the project. While every effort was made to avoid an attitude of evaluation in the observer group, it was inevitable that the therapists on the teams anxiously recalled the days when they were candidates in training and had to justify their performance to supervisors. The design of the project required that there be no communication between therapists and observers on the same team for the duration of the project; this lack of feedback and the isolation in which the observed therapists were to operate was expected to aggravate their anxieties. In order to provide some desensitization and also in order to train the observers, a number of "pilot cases" were scheduled prior to the formal start of the actual research project. Two of the therapists saw one patient each for eight observed sessions. One therapist contributed a complete psychotherapy case of sixty-eight sessions as a pilot case. Actually, except for the fact that it had not been observed in the standard manner that was later developed for the research cases, this pilot case (Case A) was completely recorded and transcribed. The patient, a young woman with a severe case of ulcerative colitis, came into psychotherapy as a last resort before contemplated surgery. She was seen sitting up twice a week for one year with several long interruptions. Therapy was terminated by mutual agreement, after the patient had been free of all symptoms for several months and was in the process of getting married and leaving town. Whle this case was not considered part of the research data, it does represent a complete record of psychotherapy.

Every hour of this case was recorded and transcribed, along with the therapist's posttherapy comments, which had been dictated immediately after every hour. Psychological tests before and after therapy and several follow-up interviews with the patient were recorded. Also, there is a brief psychotherapy report concerning the psychotherapy of the patient's husband, whom she married at the conclusion of her therapy.

The actual research data consists of two completed cases: one is "Case 101," the subject of the present volume; the other case, known as "Case #1," was the study of a case treated with classical psychoanalytic technique. The patient was a young woman whose difficult life situation and stormy transference reactions necessitated a change of therapist after the first seventy-five hours. As a result, we have the rather gratifying research situation in which there were two different therapists, a man and a woman, working with the same patient, enabling us to compare the impact of two different personalities and two different therapeutic techniques with the same patient. Because of the many complications of that case, including the necessity to shift not only therapists, but also observers, in the middle of the case, it was decided that it would be better to abandon the plan of the two cases. What we are describing in this book is the psychotherapeutic case, seen twice a week for over 100 hours. The psychoanalytic case, although completed, has not been processed for publication.

The methodology that was used in the present case will be described elsewhere in this volume. However, the history of this project would be very incomplete if some of the attempts at coping with the tremendous amounts of data were not related in some detail.

2

Review of Literature

Judd Marmor

This review of research in the therapeutic process is limited to studies of the communication, both verbal and nonverbal, between the patient and therapist, and of behavioral and personality change taking place in the patient in the course of such interaction, either during one session or over a period of time. The therapeutic modalities covered in the review include psychoanalysis, psycho-analytic-based psychotherapy, and other forms of one-to-one treatment.

Process research endeavors to impose order on what often seems to be an amorphous mass of information and expressions of feelings arising during the course of a therapeutic session or over a sequence of sessions, in the hope that we will be able, as The National Institute of Mental Health (1975) has put it, "to identify what is therapeutic about psychotherapy and what patterns of conditions enhance favorable outcomes for specific patients."

In a preliminary report on the present study, Levy (1961) described the current research plan as an intensive study of a small number of cases, each treated by a different modality of treatment, each observed by a group of psychoanalysts or research psychologists. He described the case of a young married patient undergoing psychoanalytic therapy and summarized the conclusions of the observers about the changes in the patient's behavior and symptoms during the first ten sessions and during sessions 29 to 47. He explained the hypotheses being tested as possible causes of behavioral change and stressed the importance of insight and of the interpersonal relationship between therapist and patient. He also described the transference relationship and its influence on the modification of the patient's behavior.

In a series of papers growing out of my experience in the current research project, I (Marmor 1962, 1964, 1966, and 1975) described psychoanalytic therapy as a learning process and discussed its relationship to theories of learning. I summarized the main factors in the psychotherapeutic process as (1) release of tension through catharsis and assisted by the patient's hope, faith, and expectancy, and (2) cognitive learning both of the trial and error variety and of the Gestalt variety, and (3) reconditioning through operant conditioning, including subtle reward punishment cues from the therapist as well as through corrective emotional experiences, (4) identification with the therapist, (5) repeated reality testing, which is the equivalent of practice in the learning process—all taking place under the umbrella of a supportive and empathic psychotherapeutic relationship. I suggested that these are common denominators found in all forms of psychotherapy, including psychoanalytic and others, such as those of Carl Rogers (1967) and the various behavioral schools. I wrote that I believe that suggestion and persuasion are vital to all forms of therapy and that I feel that the relationship with the therapist, both verbal and nonverbal is critical in all psychotherapeutic transactions.

There have been a number of overviews of early research on the psychotherapeutic process and of the special problems peculiar to carrying out such research. The bibliography by Strupp and Bergin (1969) is comprehensive and covers the period to 1967. Kiesler (1973), Bergin and Garfield (1971), Meltzoff and Kornreich (1970), and Gottschalk and Auerbach (1966) are other rich sources of information on what has been done in the field in earlier years. Strupp (1960) has discussed the two kinds of studies most frequently pursued. The earliest form usually consisted of the study of the single case, discussed in detail by the therapist. Most of these cases were psychoanalytic, chosen to illustrate some aspect of psychoanalytic theory. A later development of process research consisted of exhaustive statistical studies of a few variables in the therapeutic interview. Strupp expressed the hope that future studies would combine both methods, and result in research of significance and scientific validity.

Strupp and Bergin (1969) have spelled out in detail the avenues of research offering the greatest promise for understanding the psychotherapeutic process. They emphasized learning theory in particular, but also discussed other forms of influence. Their article concludes with suggestions for future research designs, including studies of therapist's variables and patient variables.

Wallerstein and Sampson (1971), Kiesler (1973), and the COPER Report of the American Psychoanalytic Association (1974) all review the special difficulties inherent in the study of the therapeutic process. Discussing this process Wallerstein and Sampson speak of the difficulties of replicating experiments, and particularly of the problems in establishing control groups in the search for cause-and-effect relationships. Schlesinger (1974) also enumerates special problems in psychoanalytic research, such as the issue of the recorded or taped interview versus the patient's right to privacy, the choice of the units and variables to be measured, and whether such variables are truely significant in the understanding of the process. He also discusses the problem of replication and of control groups against which to measure results. Luborsky and Spence (1971) review prior psychoanalytic research and especially emphasize the lack of primary data for meaningful quantitative research. Mintz and Luborsky (1971) compared the usefulness for research purposes of recording segments of interviews versus recording entire interviews. They concluded that segmented portions can offer enough for investigators to make reasonable judgments of certain aspects of the process, but that only entire recordings of interviews present the "optimal empathic relationship" between therapist and patient, an essential part of the therapeutic process. Luborsky and Spence (1971) also discuss specific problems in the collection of data on interview behavior. Obviously, memory alone, where the therapist is the sole recorder of data, is open to criticisms of possible inaccuracy and omission. Accuracy is improved through the use of recording or audiovisual electronic methods; through the use of one-way mirrors with observers; or with judges able to study transcribed tapes, with discussions of affective or kinesic responses, as well as of the verbal exchanges alone (this, of course, is precisely what our current research study has done).

Questions have been raised as to the reactions of therapists as well as of patients to the knowledge that they are being observed and their responses are being recorded. Does this affect the therapeutic process? Haggard, Hicken, and Isaacs (1965) analyzed the transcripts and recordings of cases in which both patient and therapist knew they were being recorded and/or filmed. The authors calculated the percentages of therapeutic dialogue devoted to direct or indirect reference to being observed. It was found that a control patient whose interviews were not recorded made many references to the exposure of his private feelings that were similar to those made by the research patients who were aware of the recording of their interviews.

Wallerstein and Sampson (1971) discuss the reluctance of some patients to submit to such disclosure, and the often greater reluctance of some therapists to leave themselves open to the criticism of their colleagues who are acting as observers. The authors feel however, that the inclusion of therapists as part of the research group may obviate some of their objections as well as enrich the study itself, since in that case there is the valuable ingredient of the therapist's reasonings added to the material under observation (another feature, of course, of our current study).

Dewald (1972) openly took notes during his therapeutic sessions and felt that his patient, after a brief period of self-consciousness at the procedure, apparently became oblivious to the note taking. His book is a single case study of a young woman suffering from multiple phobias, free-floating anxiety, depression, and frigidity. Verbatim accounts of many analytic sessions of a two-year analysis are followed in each instance by a discussion of the process illustrated in the session. Dewald felt that this case optimized psychoanalysis as ''a process between patient and analysts in a specifically structured situation and relationship.'' It was his conclusion that the interaction of the patient and analyst develops, explores, and finally resolves a transference neurosis and offers the patient another chance to master these conflicts that, in this case, had arrested her development and had contributed to her neurosis. In a panel on research in 1972 (Dorpat 1973) Dewald further discussed his method of research, its values, and its limitations.

Simon et al. (1970) compared the effect of observation on the analyst with that of a supervised candidate, noting many similarities, such as increased anxiety in the observed analyst, particularly when it was his turn to talk or when he became aware of the more open exposure of his countertransference reactions. Ziferstein (1971) compared his experiences in the United States, where he observed therapeutic interviews as a nonparticipant on-scene observer, and in Russia where one-way mirrors were not used and where he was often brought into the discussion when the therapist asked him direct questions. He concluded to his surprise that for both therapist and patient the interaction seemed better if the observer was not only visible but was also an occasional participant.

A number of observers have recognized that for results of research to have significance there should be a high degree of consensus among the observers as to the classification or ratings of the units under study. Therapeutic process variables, however, often are not easily categorized and individual evaluations may differ. This consensus problem has been studied by various researchers. Strupp, Chassen, and Ewing (1966) used graduate students at Vanderbilt in studies to find out the amount of training needed by observers and they present several systems for improving the definition and quantification of variables to make for greater accuracy. Luborsky et al. (1973, 1975) had psychoanalysts make ratings on twenty-three variables to show the amount of "transference" evidenced in segments of an analysis. Although there were differences, the degree of consensus on "transference" seemed high enough to justify the further use of this concept in evaluating the therapeutic process. Garfield (1974), on the other hand, found a lack of consensus among experts in deciding what variables are essential for the measurement of the therapeutic process. Obviously there is a need for more study of the choice and definition of essential variables.

A large-scale study of psychotherapy, the Menninger Foundation

Psychotherapy Research Project, was initiated in 1954, with the final results published in the *Bulletin of the Menninger Clinic* in 1972. Although the study as a whole is more concerned with patient prognosis and with therapy variables leading to favorable outcome than it is with process, the study is important in any review of research, especially, as the authors state, as "a basis for further research on issues of treatment process and treatment outcome." In the Menninger study forty-two cases were divided into groups of twelve with six cases from each group subsequently combined with six from the next. Judges compared the variables in each patient with corresponding variables in every other patient in the group and gave ratings to each. Variables studied by this "paired comparison method" included patient variables (e.g., level of anxiety, patterning of defenses, ego strength), treatment variables (e.g., interpretation, transference resolution, degree of permissiveness), and situational variables (need-congruence, interpersonal support, conflict triggers). Results of these comparisons were analyzed by computers with the aim of finding correlations between the three forms of variables and the effectiveness of different types of therapy. One of the treatment variables, transference resolution, was considered to be a measure of the therapeutic process as well as the measure of outcome. In the chapter of the report that discussed methodology concepts and findings (chap. 5) the Menninger authors discussed some of the problems of a study of this magnitude, detail, and duration, such as the attrition of many of the researchers and the tedium of performing the detailed analyses, plus such research problems as the inability to establish control groups. Despite such shortcomings, however, the authors felt that their concepts were theoretically sound. Insights gained from the study, particularly in respect to the more supportive forms of treatment with low-ego-strength patients, were incorporated into the Menninger Foundation programs (Kernberg 1972).

Robert Wallerstein's book, *Forty-Two Lives In Treatment*, 1986, is a detailed elaboration of the Menninger study with long-term follow-up. In a later paper (1988) Wallerstein reviewed some of the other prior studies, made in the 1960s, 1970s, and 1980s. A year later (1989) he discussed the project again and compared the results of psychoanalysis and of psychoanalytic psychotherapy.

Much process research embodies concentrated studies dealing with one or more variables. Marsden (1965, 1971) discussed various types of studies made of content analysis of interviews, classifying them according to whether the research was concerned with manifest or latent content of the material. He discussed some thirty different research methods. Kiesler (1973) summarized in detail seventeen of the major systems used in measuring and evaluating content of an interview and therapeutic process, the types of judges used and the amounts of their preliminary training, the codifications of the therapist's interventions, and other details. Gottschalk and Auerbach (1966) also reviewed various systems of content analysis. Some of the variables studied have been (1) observable or readily measurable aspects of the therapeutic nonverbal dialogue (e.g., pauses between responses, changes in posture), (2) types of content in the dialogue (e.g., key words, physical symptoms), (3) aspects of the psychic apparatus of the patient as revealed in the session (ego strength), (4) qualities of the therapist that affect the interaction (e.g., warmth), or (5) combinations and correlations of two or more of these factors. The work of Matarazzo and Wiens (1972) exemplifies the first of these categories. Drawing on earlier studies by Siegman and Pope (1972), they give an overview of research on utterance durations, speech interactions, ratio of therapist-to-patient offerings, and numbers and length of pauses.

A number of other researchers have emphasized the importance of such nonverbal communications as position changes, facial expressions, etc., as clues to process. Deutsch (1966) offered transcriptions of interviews, at the same time indicating the patients movements, occasional therapist's movements, and the author's interpretation of the correlation between these. Facial and body reflections of emotional reactions are studied by Dittman et al. (1965), by Scheflin (1966), and by Knapp (1974). Rice and Wagstaff (1967) studied voice quality and expressive style as indexes of productive psychotherapy.

The second category of variables was that of verbal content. Key words as indicators of emotional changes during therapy sessions were studied by Tokar and Steffler (1969) and by Gottschalk et al. (1966: 93–126, 1969) as a means of quantifying the psychoanalytic concept of affect. Chance (1966) codified verbal expressions by breaking up speeches into smaller units, then assigning the units to categories of interpersonal experiences. The books by Gottschalk and Auerbach (1966) and Kiesler (1973) review in detail the various systems of language analysis. Gottschalk's book (1966) includes work by Dollard and Auld (1959) who elaborate on their previous work *Scoring Human Motives, On Interprocesses And Sentence Coding*. White et al. (1966) also evaluated the patient's conscious motives as defined by Dollard and Auld, then studied the focus of the therapist's interventions. The authors compared the amount of discussion by a patient of a problem in early and later interviews as an indicator of the therapeutic process taking place within the patient.

Dahl (1972, 1974) and Dorpat (1973) emphasize the value of computer analysis in the study of process as revealed in language. Dahl, in his 1972 paper, codified 363 hours of the psychoanalysis into fifty-three variables and scored these by position of the hour in the total analysis, the feelings expressed, symptoms evidenced, etc. The data was analyzed by computers, and the subsequent correlations and scores demonstrate not only the process taking place in single interviews, but also changes over a period of time. In his later paper (1974), Dahl described a further use of computer analysis with a study of certain key words as they appeared in the course of twenty-five hours of an analysis.

Gottschalk (1978) and also with his associates (1975) explain how they were adapting the content analysis of speech as originally devised in the Gottschalk—Gleser Scale (1969) to computerized methods of analysis. These methods allow for more sophisticated interpretations, as analysis by trained researchers moves from single words to the parsing and scoring of whole clauses, enabling the research team to draw inferences regarding internal representations. The "hostility outward scale" has been used so far, because this scale includes easily identified action words and identifiable performers (subject nouns) and recipients (object nouns). The computer is programmed to parse and assign ratings to words in a sentence according to the amount of hostility demonstrated by the speaker toward an object.

Luborsky and Auerbach (1969) analyzed the language of a patient immediately proceeding his expression of a symptom such as headache or momentary forgetfulness. The authors analyzed the content of the communication (such as feelings of helplessness or frustration) and the possible correlation of this with the process of symptom formation.

Knapp (1974) divided interviews into segments based on (1) the time frame being discussed by the patient, such as the remote past; (2) type of experience, such as interpersonal relationships; and (3) emotional response to these. He presented a preliminary report of this work at the 1972 panel on process research (Dorpat 1973). Using part of a taped analysis, he discussed the advantages of segmenting a session along these lines, the pattern of emotions evolving from each segment giving clues to the actual stratification of affect in the patient.

Bellak, in previous studies (Bellak and Smith 1956; Bellak 1961) considered that the only variable in the analytic session was the patient himself. In a more recent paper with Sharp (1978) the authors explain a method of quantitative assessment of the patients ego function as a measure of process and progress during a psychoanalysis. They use two patients as examples, then discuss the potential of this method for a multiple case study of the psychoanalytic process. "Warded-off mental contents" comprised a variable within a patient on which Horowitz (1975) based his research. Twenty clinicans were used as judges of the material from a twenty-year-old patient. High consensus was reached on identification of warded-off contents as such material emerged in the later hours of treatment. Comparisons with content drawn from the first ten hours of these same patients demonstrated how such material had been warded off during the early sessions. The judges also agreed in their evaluations of the discomfort caused the patient and on the conditions bringing about the emergence of these themes.

Variables within the therapist or in his handling of the interview have been studied by some who considered his qualities and techniques basic to the implementation of the therapeutic process. In the 1972 discussion of research (Dorpat 1973) Merton Gill considered the effect on the psychotherapeutic process of psychoanalyst's interventions, patient's reactions, and the analyst's ways of dealing with these. In a subsequent paper, Gill and Hoffman (1982) present a method of obtaining an objective measure of the patient's experiences of the relationship with the therapist and its influence on the transference and describe a coding system for this process.

Howard and his co-workers (1968, 1976), in studies of 108 adult patients, concluding that a substantial part of the variance of their therapeutic experience was the result of differences in therapists, and the authors discussed methods of measuring these differences. A comprehensive review of research, mainly in the 1960s, on therapist's empathy, nonpossessive warmth, interpersonal skills, and the effect of these qualities on the therapeutic process in several types of psychotherapy appears in a paper by Truax and Mitchell (1971). The authors conclude that high degrees of therapist's warmth and therapist's empathy are likely to increase self-exploration in patients and to foster progress in the psychotherapeutic process. Meltzoff and Kornreich (1970) also reviewed research of this subject and reached similar conclusions.

How do patients and therapists feel about the therapeutic process and the changes taking place as a result of therapy? Is psychotherapy, as Mintz and his colleagues (1973) found it, a "Rashomon" experience, in which one's judgement of the process and satisfactory nature of the session depend on whether one is the patient, the therapist, or an observer?

Orlinsky (Orlinsky and Howard 1967) and his co-worker Howard (Howard, Onlinsky, and Hill 1968, 1969; Howard, Orlinsky, and Perlstein 1976) compared patients and therapists' judgements of the experience of psychotherapy and of what takes place in the "good" or "bad" therapy hour. Many factors, such as the amount of embarrassment or disagreeable emotion elicited, may influence the patient's view of the process. A "bad" session to the therapist may mean a dull one. Other variables include the style of relating between participants and the topics discussed.

Hoffman and Gill (1988) discussed their coding schemes for transcripts of audio-recorded sessions, and compared these with schemas used by other researchers. Ka'chele (1988) reviewed the UIM process model of psychoanalysis. In this study sessions conducted by one analyst were monitored by another and a study was made of the influence of theory on the clincans handling of the analysis. Luborsky and Crits-Cristoph (1988) described and evaluated their methods of measuring three concepts effecting process in the so-called Penn Studies: (1) the therapeutic alliance, (2) transference patterns, and (3) accuracy of interpretations. Weiss (1988) discussed his methods of testing unconscious mental functioning during psychoanalytic sessions. The Penn Project was also discussed by Luborsky et al. (1980) with regard to its ability to predict outcome. Crits-Cristoph (1988) also discussed this from the viewpoint of the accuracy of the therapist's interpretations and their effect on outcome. The book *Who Will Benefit From Psychotherapy*, Luborsky and Crits-Cristoph et al (1988), gives further details of the Penn Project and elaborates on predictive factors in the patient and therapist and the quality that is needed from each for patient improvement.

Weiss and Sampson in their book, *The Psychoanalytic Process* (1986) elaborate on their work in the Mount Zion Psychotherapy Research Project which Weiss began in 1968, joining forces with Sampson in 1964 and organizing a group in 1972. One hundred sessions of single cases were audiotaped, transcribed, and then analyzed in randomly selected sections by a group of judges. Their special interest was in warded-off (unconscious) content. The results confirmed the theory of repressed material and the patient's part in the emergence of this material during treatment. The authors discuss this subject again in a chapter of Masling's book *Empirical Studies Of Psychoanalytic Theories* (Weiss and Sampson 1986). In volume 1 of the same book Hartly and Strupp (1983) discuss the therapeutic alliance and its possible relationship to outcome. Strupp summarizes his views in an article, "Psychotherapy: Can the Practitioner Learn From the Researcher?" (1989) in which he challenges criticisms and cites his Vanderbilt studies as well as those made by other groups as proving the worth of research on the field.

Frank in his classic volume *Persuasion and Healing* (1973) also emphasized the patient-therapist relationship as vital to the therapeutic process. He also described experiments on persuasion performed on college sophomores but issued some caveats in comparing such experiments to real-life situations in which the patient rather than an experimentor chooses the problem to be worked on.

Other papers on the subject of research on therapist variables have been done by Parloff et al. (1978), by Howard et al. (Howard,

Orlinsky, and Trattner 1970; Howard, Orlinsky, and Perlstein 1976), by Truax and Mitchell (1971) and Meltzoff and Kornreich (1970).

A book edited by Donald Freedheim *The History Of Psychotherapy: A Century Of Change*, (1992), devotes a large section to developments in psychotherapy research. A section by Strupp and Howard (1992) describes the founding in 1970, of the Society for Psychotherapy Research with over one thousand members from twenty-seven countries. The format suggested by the Peer Review Committee set up by NIMH to assist in the processing of grant applications is discussed together with other developments. There are brief descriptions of eight separate research groups. In a subsequent chapter, a number of well-known research projects are described by persons closely allied with them. These include: the Johns Hopkins Psychotherapy Project described by Jerome Frank (1992), the Penn Research Project, discussed by Lester Luborsky, the Menninger Foundation Psychotherapy Research Project described by Robert Wallerstein, the Mount Zion Group described by Howard Sampson and Joseph Weiss and the Vanderbilt Center discussed by William Henry and Hans Strupp plus other research studies discussed by Bergin, Horowitz and Parloff. Another publication by Beutler and Crago (1991) covers large-scale programs in centers in both North America and Europe.

What are the current trends in research on the therapeutic process? Omer and Dar (1992) reviewed three decades of such research and concluded that the trend has turned away from rigid schools and systems, perhaps, in their opinion, going too far in the opposite direction. They hold the hope that future research will remain close to real clinical traditions and provide the link between credible outcome criteria and theory-guided process measures. They feel that detailed case studies still offer promise to the researcher.

Beutler and Machado (1992) feel that psychotherapy research has gone through three phases: (1) case analysis, (2) descriptive assessment, and (3) controlled experiments. They suggest that future researchers face a fourth, more mature phase, "characterized by methods that are designed to address complex interactions among treatment, patient, outcome, and process variables." In essence, this is precisely what the present research study has addressed itself to!

3

Methodology

The problem of methodology was the major concern of our team of investigators throughout the first year of the project. Although we had agreed on the basic concept that both the psychotherapeutic case and the psychoanalytic case would be observed by teams of psychoanalysts, the question of how and what to observe, as well as how and what to record, proved to be an extremely knotty one. There was no difficulty, of course, about the verbal material. That was to be recorded in any event, and a permanent transcript of the verbal transactions of each hour would be preserved. The nonverbal material, however, presented a difficult problem. There were some within the investigating team that wanted to make a record of every nonverbal transaction to the fullest possible extent. They advocated recording not merely obvious facial expressions and emotional reactions, but also more minute movements of every part of the body that was observable in both patient and therapist. For a while, indeed, an effort was made to see whether such a record could be kept, but it soon became apparent that this would involve the amassment of mountains of data that would utterly defy any subsequent efforts at processing.

Other variations of observation were attempted during the pilot phase. Thus, one observer tried listening only to the voices without watching, in order to more effectively focus on changes of vocal expression. Another tried shutting off the sound and focusing only on the facial reactions, in the hope that he would thereby be less distracted from picking up subtle nonverbal communications of expression or movement. One observer tried focusing only on the patient, another only on the therapist; but after this kind of experimentation had gone on for several weeks, it became obvious that more was being lost than gained by such fragmentation of observation. It became increasingly clear that the thing that gave the greatest meaning to the therapeutic process, as it was observed from the outside, was the *gestalt of the total patient-therapist transaction*, and this, therefore, had to be viewed in its totality.

The conclusion finally arrived at by the overwhelming majority of the team members, therefore, was that the observational process should be both aural and visual and that the observers should use their customary observational techniques and experience as therapists to try to grasp everything that was going on in the patient-therapist transaction that they considered significant, and to focus on the gestalt of the total transaction rather than on minute isolated facets of it. For this purpose an observer's work sheet was constructed (see Appendix) that gave the observer an opportunity to record these observations and impressions in a uniform and organized way. The therapist, as well as each observer, filled out one of these work sheets immediately following each session. Special care was taken to avoid communication between the therapist and his observers, or between the observers themselves, in order to avoid the possibility of their influencing one another's observations and evaluations.

Parenthetically, the construction of the work sheet itself was by no means a simple matter. Many hours of discussion went into its elaboration—discussion not only about what should go into it, but also about the precise meaning of the various items listed.

The initial item (*I Observer as a Person*) gave the observer the opportunity to comment on his own physical and affective state at the time.

The second item (*II Free Style Account of the Hour*) asked for a running account of the entire session in as much detail as the observer could recall using his notes taken during the observational period. This was expected to include not merely the content of the hour in terms of verbal interchange, but also any concommitant nonverbal actions and reactions on the part of the therapist and the patient.

The subsequent items dealt with the major assumptions being tested in the investigation, in order to permit a systematic recording of data relevant to these assumptions.

The next section, (*III Events of the Hour*), included the main themes discussed (by therapist and/or patient); what topics were evaded and focused upon and by whom; discrepancies between manifest verbal content and nonverbal behavior; and points of highest emotional intensity. The final item in this section dealt with what was termed *style*. This referred to the *manner* in which therapist and patient expressed themselves and communicated with one another. Their customary style became a baseline from which deviations and fluctuations could be easily noted.

The next section (*IV Interventions*) dealt with the therapist's major interventions, the manner in which they were made, and the patient's reactions to them. Nonverbal factors such as tone of voice, quality of emotion, etc., were significant here also.

In the following section, (*V Therapist as a Person*), the observers recorded their observations about the therapist's affective state and his main emotional attitudes during the hour, with special emphasis on his nonverbal as well as verbal reactions. Whenever possible, they made naturalistic inferences from the therapist's words and actions about his wishes, hopes, and expectations, his approvals and disapprovals, his feeling—gratified or frustrated, critical or angry, bored or interested—in relation to the patient, at any particular point in the hour. Any factual information revealed by the therapist concerning his attitudes, values, personal life, etc., were also recorded here. No attempt was made to label the therapists' attitudes in technical language but simply to identify and describe them and to note their motivation in relation to the events of the hour, or possibly to events outside of the hour.

In the next section (*VI Intrapersonal Processes*) observations about intrapsychic processes in the patient were recorded. These included

1. the main conflicts, the main unconscious tendencies, the resistances, and the defenses being used;
2. transference manifestations;

3. evidences of imitation and/or identification with the therapist;
4. new or increased awarenesses (insight) both cognitive and emotional.

The final section (*VII Shifts and Changes*) pertained to significant changes noted in the patient's basic behavior, attitudes, or symptoms, both qualitatively and quantitatively.

In addition to these naturalistic observations, an effort was made, initially, to record physiological changes in both therapist and patient. Polygraphic recordings of pulse rate, respiratory rate, and galvanic skin reactions were obtained for some of the sessions in Case 101, but finally had to be discontinued because of both technical and personnel problems. It is worth noting, however, that the various wirings attached to the wrists and fingers did not seem to affect to a great extent the functioning of either therapist or patient in the therapeutic transaction, at least during the brief period in which it was utilized.

An effort was made, in addition, to try to have the therapist instantaneously record his own subjective reactions as he experienced them in the therapeutic situation. This was done by constructing a keyboard with five buttons, easily available to the therapist's left hand. One button was to deal with physical sensations; e.g., sleepiness or drowsiness, one push of the button; any other physical symptoms, two pushes. A "feeling" button—erotic sensation, one push; irritability, two pushes; empathy, commiseration, etc., three pushes. A third button was to deal with "thoughts about self" and was to be pushed whenever the therapist became aware that he had been thinking about events relating to his own life, for example, thoughts about the past, one push; thoughts about the present, two pushes; about the future, three pushes. A fourth button was to deal with insights, and the therapist was to push it at that moment at which he became aware of a specific insight about the patient. The fifth button was to deal with any thoughts or awarenesses of the observers.

However, although the idea in and of itself was a worthwhile one, it presented problems that proved insuperable. Although it is possible that with a sufficiently prolonged period of training, a therapist might learn to record such data more or less automatically, in practice it proved to be (and probably always would be) so great a barrier to the therapist's ability to concentrate on the patient, that it had to be discarded as a serious impediment to the naturalness and spontaneity of the therapeutic procedure.

Physical Setup of the Study

The physical setting for the study consisted of a special sound-proofed consultation room surrounded by four observation booths provided with one-way mirrors, enabling the occupants to see into the consultation room. The recording equipment was in an adjacent area.

The consulting room contained a patient's couch, an easy chair for the therapist, and a coffee table, arranged so that both patient and therapist could be clearly seen by all the observers. The microphone, which was concealed, fed into tape recorders, and into headphones in each of the observation booths. Thus, observers were enabled to simultaneously hear and see what was going on in the consultation room. Initially, each observation booth was equipped with a microphone so that the observer could make comments simultaneously with his observation. However, this was found to be impractical since the use of the microphone by the observers interfered with their capacity to pay continuous auditory attention to what was going on between therapist and patient. Consequently, the method finally arrived at was that of having the observers write notes on special sheets on which the time sequences were recorded on the left hand edge of the sheet (see Appendix). To facilitate this technique, a time signal was spoken each minute during the session, into the sound system so that the observer's comments or notes could be synchronized with the time signal on the therapist's-patient's tape. When the typed verbatim transcripts of each session was made, this was also made on paper on which each minute and each ten seconds was marked. This enabled the observers subsequently to recheck their own observations against the actual recorded transcript. What the observers did, therefore, was to make continuous notes based on their auditory and visual observations of the patient-therapist transaction. Then, immediately following each observation session, the observer would dictate onto a tape or to a secretary his observations and impressions, following the organization of the observer's work sheet already referred to.

The consultation room was also equipped with a one-way mirror designed for a motion picture camera. However, the use of filmed interviews was not part of the present research design because of the considerable cost involved.* The consultation and observation rooms were arranged in such a way, moreover, that the observation rooms and their occupants were concealed by doors from the patient as he came and went. The observers were required to abstain from smoking, as the glowing tip of a cigarette or cigar would be visible through the one-way mirror to the therapist and patient.

The first year of the project, from January to December 1957, was devoted to working out and testing observational techniques and categories, as well as procedures for collecting and recording the data. This included a test case consisting of the psychoanalytic psychotherapy of a case of ulcerative colitis, already mentioned.

One of the primary concerns of the research team throughout was the question of the reliability of the data obtained. Verbal communication with the patient and therapist presented no problem since they could be recorded permanently on tape and subsequently typed out. The use of human beings, however, as observational and recording instruments concerning the nonverbal communications presented a particular difficulty. We were aware that the conscious and particularly the unconscious attitudes of the observers inevitably influence both their perceptions and their observations. The use of three independent observers in each case represented an effort to minimize this human factor and to increase the reliability of the data. The therapists as well as the observers were all experienced psychoanalysts. Special care was taken that the observers did not communicate with each other about the case that they were mutually observing, in order to prevent their influencing one another. Equal care was taken, also, to prevent any communication between the observers and the therapist.

---

*Videotape techniques were not available at that time.

Evaluation of the Methodology

One of the methodological problems that arose in the study was that all members of the observing team, as psychoanalytically trained psychiatrists, shared to some extent the same basic theoretical models of psychodynamic intra- and interpersonal processes. Obviously, the nature of the observations were necessarily affected by this. In an effort, however, to avoid the use of jargon that might conceal ambiguities of meaning, a conscious effort was made by all of the observers to describe the overt interpersonal emotional interactions in the ordinary language of everyday human relations, rather than in technical language. Having made their descriptions as unambiguous as possible, however, they were then free to add inferences about the covert preconscious and unconscious emotional processes involved, inferences based on their particular psychodynamic understanding.

Apart from the reliability of the data themselves, however, a number of other questions arose concerning the research project. The most obvious one was the question of whether the fact of being observed does not alter the very nature of the psychotherapeutic process. The conclusion to which both therapists and observers all arrived was that this observational process did not materially affect the nature of the psychotherapeutic process. Initially, both therapist and patient were aware of the observation teams and experienced some discomfort. Curiously enough, it was the therapist more than the patient who tended to remain somewhat aware of the observing team. This awareness, however, did not genuinely interfere with his therapeutic approach; on the contrary, it tended to heighten his efforts to function effectively, for fear of being criticized by his colleagues. On some occasions, the therapists were aware of "performing" for their colleagues, but for the most part this was not a significant factor. As far as the patients were concerned, it became clear that after the first few hours, both patients were reporting their experiences and feelings as freely as patients we had all had in our private offices. The observers made a conscious effort to remain aware of the tendency to compare the observed therapy with their own individual therapeutic model, and also made a consistent effort to avoid sitting in judgment of the therapist-colleague.

Another important element of the research design was the comparison of the observations and evaluations of the therapeutic process by the therapist and by the observing team. The purpose of this was to obtain data relevant to our hypotheses that the therapist as a participant observer will at times fail to make adequate observations about his own actions and attitudes and about the interpersonal interaction between himself and the patient. This comparison is described in chapter 12. The original plan was to subsequently have a meeting between the therapist and the observing team during which they would have an opportunity to examine and discuss their respective reports. It was hoped that certain important data would be obtained from this procedure. The therapist would have an opportunity to give information about some of his conscious motives and purposes for particular actions and interventions that would shed additional light on them and might induce the team to modify certain of its inferences and thus result in a more accurate understanding of the therapeutic processes. This opportunity to identify and discuss the differences in their perception of and inferences about the therapeutic events, which was potentially very productive, unfortunately could not be carried out completely, due to events over which we had no control. As will be seen, however, the section in which the therapist responds to the team presentation illustrates sharply some of the differences in how the therapeutic process was perceived by the therapist and by the external observers.

4

Processing of the Data

As described above, the raw data consisted of the tapes, the verbatim transcript, and the posthour work sheets of the individual observers and of the therapist. One member of the team, designated "the coordinator,"* was assigned the task of developing a description of each therapeutic session (the "coordinator report"), utilizing the work sheets of the observers, the therapist, and the verbatim report. This description, based on the verbal communications of patient and therapist, and on the observations and inferences reported by the observers (the nonverbal elements in the transaction), plus data from the therapist's work sheet, was thus a synthesis of all the reports. Inextricably interwoven in this synthesis were the inferences made by the coordinator himself as he worked over the verbal transcripts and work sheets. The coordinator found that it was necessary to devote at least several days to process one therapy session, as it was not possible to grasp the subtle elements in the nonverbal and verbal communications in a single reading. He found he had to allow a period of time to consciously, and to some extent preconsciously, work over the encounter between patient and therapist.

The next step in the processing was the report of the observing team. The description of the therapy was divided into a series of blocks of sessions as follows: Session 1–10, 11–21, 22–28, 29–47,

---

*Although the coordinator was not one of the regular observers, he observed a number of sessions.

48–64, 65–80, 81–98. These were determined predominantly by interruptions in the therapy but also for convenience in processing. This phase of processing was done by the team consisting of the three observers and the coordinator and an integrated conclusion was agreed upon. The coordinator's reports of the sessions were now the main source of data, but the original raw data was consulted as needed and as indicated. The observer's report consisted of the following sections (see next chapter):

1. Summary of Manifest Events
2. Therapist-Patient Interaction
3. The Therapeutic Experience of the Patient
   A.   In the interpersonal relationship with the therapist
   B.   New or increased awareness (insights)
   C.   Symptomatic and/or behavioral changes.

A brief description of these sections, which are on the whole self-explanatory, might be helpful. The purpose of the Section 1, Summary of Manifest Events, is to give the reader a summary of the main overt, manifest, observable events of each session in the block. We hope the reader will have a reasonably clear overall picture of the main events in the therapeutic encounter, that is, the main actions of both therapist and patient, and the main foci of the verbal communications.

Section 2, the Therapist-Patient Interaction, requires little explanation. It represents the inferences drawn by the team about the overt and the covert interactional process, including both transference and nontransference elements. An effort was made to avoid inferences about psychodynamic processes that were not close to the observable verbal and nonverbal phenomena.

Section 3, The Therapeutic Experience of the Patient, was an attempt to describe what the team regarded as the experience the patient was having in this therapeutic encounter. This was an analysis consisting of inferences about conscious and nonconscious emotional reactions as well as the cognitive-intellectual experience. The items of new and increased awarenesses, and the symptomatic and behavioral changes are self-evident.

The three sections were divided up between the team members for processing. The entire team then met and went over each section sentence by sentence. An attempt was made to reach as much consensus as possible, as team members sometimes disagreed about particular points. Each member would refer to the data as evidence to support his view. In most instances a consensus could be reached. When it could not, the differing views were explicitly stated in the report. It is our impression that we achieved greater reliability with this procedure, as it made it necessary for each member to re-scrutinize the data whenever there was a disagreement. In many instances this would lead to a revision of a team member's conclusion, not out of compliance or the desire to achieve a consensus, but on the basis of a genuine re-evaluation. We realize, of course, that there is a danger inherent in such a procedure, as the seeking of consensus may lead to premature or unwarranted rejection of a valid difference.

5

Anamnesis

The patient presented himself for screening in December 1957 as an applicant for psychotherapy in the Ford Project for the Study of the Psychotherapeutic Process. He was a thirty-five-year-old, married, white, Protestant male, who had two sons, one aged four years and the other fifteen months. He had a brother one year older, and a sister seven years younger. During the past seven years he had been employed as a psychologist in various clinics. He was meticulously dressed, well-groomed, and clean-cut in features. He radiated a nervous high-pitched vitality. He was articulate, superior in intelligence, and psychologically sophisticated. His mood reflected much self-dissatisfaction. His complaints referred both to emotional and physical insufficiencies, and he professed a strong urge to get help.

Chief Complaints

When first seen, the patient complained of "tension states" manifested in anxiety attacks, headaches, and recurrent episodes of sexual impotence.

He had initially sought treatment in May 1957 with a psychiatrist, Dr. A., because of feelings of anxiety, elevated blood pressure, and recurrent states of depression. He had developed "tension headaches," which had been growing progressively worse for three months. They were accompanied by tingling sensations in his feet, tightness in his face, and almost constant numbness in his left arm.

Inasmuch as he was unable to afford individual psychotherapy, he agreed to try group therapy twice weekly. According to the patient he felt "wonderful" during his first month of treatment with Dr. A. His anxiety states and headaches diminished, and his systolic blood pressure readings dropped from the 140–160mm range to normal.

However, the group then began to confront him with what they perceived as his monopolistic, competitive, and demanding attitudes. He became resentful when a group member told him, "You want to be a boy again; you want your wife to be your mother." He protested that he was being unfairly attacked, discriminated against, and not being given enough time in the group sessions. He expressed jealousy that some patients were getting individual sessions of therapy while he wasn't. In July 1957, five or six weeks after the beginning of treatment, he experienced a sudden onset of impotence. As it persisted, his anxiety mounted to panic proportions. He felt demoralized, his need for more time in the group increased, and rivalry feelings toward other group members intensified. There were angry exchanges, especially between him and an overt homosexual in the group. The patient became convinced that group therapy was worsening his condition, and not providing him with sufficient support. The therapist agreed to discontinue group sessions. A few individual consultations ensued during which the patient's panic subsided to tolerable proportions, but since he was not able to afford continued individual treatment, therapy was then terminated. The patient was dejected and very depressed for about three weeks but then began to feel better, although his tension symptoms and impotence persisted without respite.

Past History

The patient was born in a large eastern city when his mother was twenty-one and his father twenty-five. He was told that his mother almost died of a postpartum peritonitis, and also that she had been so set on having a daughter that in a fit of rage she burned all of her new infant's diapers. He described his mother as warm, but highly emotional, loud-voiced, and explosive in temper. She henpecked and bossed all the males in her family. She was generous and talented, but demanded acceptance on her own terms. She took pride in maintaining an efficient household. The patient's father was described as a struggling traveling salesman, barely able to make ends meet. Basically mild-mannered, he was, however, able to generate considerable stubbornness in the face of his wife's bossiness, and resisted her demands that he take up a better line of work. Although warm to his children he was never "buddy-buddy" with them. The mother accused her husband of being an unreliable, irresponsible man who treated her badly. She frequently exhorted her sons to take her side against him, which they did. The mother's father was also described by her as an irresponsible character who had been in jail and whose wife (mother's mother) was "martyred" and gave him "dog-life" love.

From the time that the patient was age three to five, the family lived with the paternal grandparents in another state. There was great strife; the grandmother accused the patient's mother of being unfit and tried to break up the marriage, until the mother took the sons and fled to another town where they soon were rejoined by the father. The mother never forgave the grandmother and held it against her husband as well.

Shortly after, the mother's two younger married brothers began to live with them. She came into conflict with their wives, which resulted in painful grievances with her brothers also. The patient feels that he was treated by his mother in the same way that she treated the older of her two brothers.

When the patient was seven, his sister was born. The mother seemed to allow unlimited freedom, aggression, and spontaneity to the girl while keeping close rein on the boys, insisting they be quiet, well-behaved, and clean. The patient, conforming with his mother's wishes, idealized his sister, treating her like a princess and elevating her on a pedestal. The sons also fulfilled the mother's expectations that they excel in school. Until he was thirteen, both the patient and his brother idolized their mother and considered her always right. At this time the continuing economic depression caused great difficulties in the family, and there was constant fighting between the parents over money. Even though the sons loved their father, they took the mother's side in the fights, as she enlisted their support in making the father feel like a "louse." However, gradually the boys became more observant, and more critical of the mother's attitudes. The patient began to stutter, especially on the word "mother." This began at age thirteen after an incident in which she beat and kicked him. When he presented himself for therapy, however, he no longer stuttered but did occasionally lapse into a suggestion of lisping.

At about sixteen, the patient and his older brother began to participate more in social activities, joining clubs, and dating, with mother growing increasingly critical of them. Upon graduating from high school his brother was allowed to attend day college, but when patient graduated he was forced to go to work to contribute to the support of the family and to take his schooling by attending night school. For three-and-a-half years he worked in the garment industry, resenting the menial work, while accumulating two years of college credits and unhappy that his brother was "taking it easy."

Military History

At the age of twenty the patient entered military service for three years as a radio technologist. At the end of this period, the brother, who was also in the service, was given the choice of going home and took it. The patient felt deeply aggrieved, abandoned, rejected, and betrayed. He was furious at what he considered to be his brother's selfish behavior of leaving him in the service by himself.

At the age of twenty-three the patient was also mustered out, whereupon he resumed his education, full-time, choosing clinical psychology as his career. He excelled in his studies and his self-confidence and self-esteem grew apace. He embarked on his first sexual affair. There was a false alarm about pregnancy, but he successfully resisted the girl's efforts to marry him. The following year, while visiting his brother, who was a student at a European university, he discovered to his surprise, and with considerable satisfaction, that his brother was having a really tough struggle, while the patient had been doing marvelously well. Patient continued this successful performance even to the extent of being, as he put it, with a tinge of self-mockery, the "fair-haired boy" of his class.

He graduated at the age of twenty-eight and married the following year after a brief courtship of two months. Worthy of note is the fact that this decision was made on the heels of learning that his mother was scheduled for an exploratory operation for a possible malignancy. He wavered inwardly when it turned out to be benign, but he went through with the marriage anyway.

Work History

In his first job from 1951 to 1955, the patient performed very well and was pleased with his progress. However, his ambitions were seriously frustrated when after several years he was refused a promotion on the grounds that he was too aggressive and unsuitable for a supervisory position, probably because he was always rebelling against administrative policies. Patient's disappointment, hurt feelings, anger, and rivalry with his colleagues led him to resign from this position.

He spent the following year, 1955–1956, at another clinic. Here he felt isolated and lonely and thrown entirely on to his own resources. In part, he was unhappy, also, because he ran into conflict with a colleague. He began to suffer from symptoms of depression, dizziness, throbbing headaches, and anxiety. He felt sick and his physician told him he had an elevated systolic blood pressure. However, in the summer of 1956, one-and-a-half years before being seen at the Ford Project, he obtained a position at another clinic where his status and self-respect improved. There were ample opportunities for professional interchange with respected colleagues and much stimulus for professional growth and achievement.

History of Present Illness

Impotency was the major concern of the patient when he was first interviewed in December 1957 at the Ford Project. Except for a transitory problem of mild premature ejaculation in the first year of marriage, there had been no sexual problem of this nature until the rather sudden onset of impotence, which appeared in mid-July of 1957 and had persisted to the present time. In discussing the onset of his sexual impotence, the patient stated that he was not getting along with his mother, who displayed a chronic resentment against him. He also was having difficulties in adjusting to his marriage and to his felt need to live his own life.

This tension with his mother came to a head in January 1957, around New Year's Eve, when his four-month-old infant had a severe attack of bronchitis. Unable to reach a doctor, he called his mother to stay with the four-year-old son so they could take the baby to the hospital. The mother, who had already retired, displayed reluctance, and sarcastically minimized his concern for the baby's condition. The patient finally found a doctor who would come to the house and phoned his mother, but she was already dressed, and with annoyance insisted on coming anyway. When the case was diagnosed as rather serious, his mother became alarmed that the baby might die and the atmosphere, charged on all sides by now, exploded. His mother criticized the patient and his wife for using clinic doctors. The wife was furious because his mother had neglected the older child, while the mother angrily accused the wife of alienating her son and his children from her, and of making her son sick. Shouting and yelling, the mother and wife became hysterical. The patient was numbed and horrified at his mother's assault on his wife, who he knew had wanted so much to have his mother replace her own who had died four years earlier. He finally intervened, trying to calm his wife who had retired to the bathroom where she had fainted. Upon recovering, she ran to look at a picture of her mother, trying to console herself. The patient's guilt was now further enhanced when his wife accused him of failing to take her side against his mother. At his wife's insistence, thereafter, they almost completely broke off seeing his mother.

The second incident of note occurred about six months later, about one week before the onset of his impotence. At the instigation of his wife he agreed to have a "mature" talk with his mother in an effort at reconciliation. His mother complained that his father was treating her badly and that he (the patient) was letting her down in not taking her side. This the patient flatly refused to do. He told her that his father was "really a nice guy" and that she was expecting too much of him. Although he called it a draw, the patient was exhilarated at this first experience in standing up to his mother and even telling her off. A week later, however, when his wife criticized him during intercourse of taking too much time, he became impotent, and this had persisted until the time of his seeking treatment at the Ford Project.

6

Therapy—Sessions 1–10

Summary of Manifest Events

Session No. 1 (9 January 1958)

The verbal communications of the initial hour deal primarily with the circumstances surrounding the onset of patient's symptoms of sexual impotence, tension headaches and hypertension. Therapist requests this explicitly for the benefit of the observers, although he himself has received this information in a previous interview. Patient cooperates compliantly.

Session No. 2 (13 January 1958)

Patient begins the second hour by indicating how much the treatment means to him. He expresses a fear of "opening up" lest he be rejected by therapist, expresses some concern about who the observers are, and asks for and receives reassurance that he is acceptable to the project and that the therapeutic management of his case is entirely in therapist's own hands.

The rest of the hour consists mainly of the presentation of anamnestic material as requested by therapist. Therapist interrupts from time to time with various confrontations and interpretations about family interrelationships.

Session No. 3 (16 January 1958)

Patient speaks of his continued impotence, his annoyance with his wife for not being as intellectually sophisticated as he would like, and elaborates his feelings about his mother and his wife's mother, whom he describes as a rather nagging and dominating woman also. In his relationship to therapist, patient seems more relaxed, leans closer to therapist, and shows clear indications of a developing positive transference and the beginnings of a working alliance.

Therapist becomes very active and makes numerous interpretations. Therapist's interpretations are that patient's impotence is connected with (1) conflict betweeen unconscious dependent needs and his conscious wish to be a man; (2) conflict over resentment toward his wife for wanting him to be a man and satisfy her dependent needs; and (3) conflict between a wish for a mother and a wish to be independent of mother. Patient expresses verbal acceptance of therapist's interpretations but tense silences suggest that he may be emotionally disturbed by them.

Session No. 4 (20 January 1958)

In the fourth hour, patient reveals a tendency toward a submissive adaptation to therapist's great activity of the previous hour. He expresses a fear of showing anger lest he lose support and states that the previous session had cast a "floodlight" on his problem by focusing on his "selfishness." At the same time, repressed aggressiveness is suggested by his technique of asking repeated questions and reacting with a kind of "psychogenic pseudo-stupidity."

The central manifest theme of this hour is patient's relationship with his brother, and his painful realization that his brother does not reciprocate his love. Therapist's interpretations focus on the theme of patient's dependent needs, hostility, resultant guilt, and fear of rejection. Therapist's feelings are revealed in his frequent characterization of patient as "soft," and it is implicit that he wishes patient to become a tougher, harder, and more masculine person.

Session No. 5 (23 January 1958)

The central manifest theme of this hour is patient's description of a situation at a previous job where he had failed to get an anticipated promotion. He attributes this to his tendency to identify himself with the underdog against the administrative authorities. Therapist interprets patient's revolt against authority as unconsciously motivated by a wish to be bullied and to remain dependent, and states that even though patient resents being an underdog, he has a need to remain one, and feels uncomfortable in any situation in which he is not. Therapist's attitude is pressuring and rather critical.

Patient then reports a dream in which his father died, but patient didn't really care. The transference implications of this dream are touched upon but not explored. The implication that patient is reacting with repressed anger at therapist for the latter's deprecatory attitudes to him is reinforced by the fact that toward the end of the session when therapist implies to patient that he is "not a man," patient flares up for the first time and expresses anger. In the face of this, therapist retreats and indicates that what he meant by "man" was a "mature person." Patient ends session by saying, "I'm glad we got this clarified."

Session No. 6 (27 January 1958)

Patient is smiling and cheerful at the beginning of the session, reports he has been feeling much better after the previous visit, and even sexually desirous. He comments that therapist must have thrown "some magic stuff" at him last time. He then launches into a discussion that centers on his relationships with the various women in his life—his mother, his wife, his sisters-in-law, and his supervisor. Therapist interprets patient's relationship to the mother as the "soft point" in his problem and says that all else is derivative. On the basis of patient's own material, therapist points out that he must be hostile to women, but patient resists the interpretation. Therapist suggests that patient's hostility to women creates guilt, which then enhances his sensitivity to their criticism.

In contrast to the previous hour, therapist's attitude to patient is relatively objective, nonpressuring and not deprecatory, and patient in turn cooperates fully in the intellectual explorations.

Session No. 7 (30 January 1958)

In this hour, patient and therapist continue to explore intellectually what it is that is preventing patient from accepting the idea of "chronic hostility to women." The chief focus is on his relationships to his wife and his mother. Therapist continues to present repeated psychodynamic formulations that patient represses his hostility because he has a fear of being rejected; also that he clings to the weak role and repudiates the role of the "husband, father, man, and adult" as a way of avoiding the responsibilities that go with these roles, and of justifying his wish to remain dependent.

Therapist's attitude in this session appears cool, impersonal, and somewhat unempathic. That he is not totally unaware of patient's sensitivities, however, is indicated when he laughingly adds the words "and adult" to his comment that patient is repudiating the role of "husband, father, and man." Patient reports that he is continuing to feel better, more alive, more confident, less depressed. Therapist terminates both this and the previous session five minutes early, something he has not previously done.

Session No. 8 (3 February 1958)

Patient reports being depressed and anxious since the previous session. His remarks focus chiefly on feelings of depreciation by his mother, his brother, and various professional colleagues. (Significantly, he does not refer to feeling depreciated by therapist.) His complaints reach a high point after about seventeen minutes, when he complains of feeling utterly useless, helpless, and impotent, and becomes tearful. Therapist responds to this with impatience. He confronts patient forcefully with not wanting to give up his symptoms, with exaggerating them, with trying to get sympathy with them; and compares him with a "complaining martyr wife." He attributes patient's return of symptoms to a "stubborn recrudescence," "almost spitefully pulled out," and indicates that patient could have had (and by implication should have had) an opposite reaction of "daring to feel like a man." He suggests that patient ought to tell his mother and brother "to go to Hell."

Patient's response to all of this is essentially submissive. He appears hurt, tense, sad, and overwhelmed. He makes a few feeble efforts to disagree with therapist, but is overriden by the latter's forceful pressure. He leaves, however, with the comment that he has been given "a lot to think about."

Session No. 9 (6 February 1958)

Patient appears cheerful and self-confident. His depressive reaction of the previous session is gone. He reports that they hit "pay dirt" the previous time, that he has been feeling better, has been able to assert himself with his wife, and that his sexual libido and potency have returned. The ensuing intellectual discussion revolves around repressed anger as the source of his feelings of tension. Therapist points out that patient's repressed anger leads to feelings of depression, impotence, and submissiveness, which then lead to increased anger and so to a vicious cycle. Patient accepts and intellectually confirm's therapist's formulations. Therapist appears friendlier and is distinctly less pressuring than he has been in the previous session.

Session No. 10 (10 February 1958)

The central manifest theme of this session is patient's reaction of humiliation and rage, when Mrs. B., a colleague, asked him to give up his seat at lunch to a female teacher. He subsequently took out his rage against his wife, and also became impotent again with her that evening. Therapist interprets patient's behavior as an overreaction, points out his displacement of anger to his wife, his use of sex to prove his masculinity, and his development of impotence as a self-punishment, in part at least, for the anger he felt. He gives patient fatherly advice about how to be sophisticatedly aggressive in a social situation and also suggests that he should not attempt to have sexual relations unless he feels a definitive physiological urge. Therapist continues to make occasional critical remarks about patient but generally softens his comments with friendly laughter when making them. After some initial disagreement, patient accepts therapist's interpretations as correct, his feelings of anger and humiliation disappear, and he leaves feeling cheerful and relieved.

Therapist-Patient Interaction

The relationship is a professional one, with both patient and therapist remaining in their respective roles consistently. They are in the sitting position in comfortable chairs facing each other. There is much active interaction and verbal exchange. Therapist is for the most part active and consistently demonstrates by verbal and nonverbal behavior his continuous and strong interest in achieving an intellectual understanding of the dynamics of patient's symptoms and behavior. This is a conscious striving of the therapist as stated in his worksheet. Patient also has a conscious desire for intellectual understanding, and readily participates in the work with therapist. Patient reveals from the beginning an eager, somewhat childlike, deferential attitude toward therapist. His manner is often whining and pleading. Therapist usually takes the lead and seems to have strong desires for patient to acquire the insights which he, therapist, considers important.

Patient, in turn, cooperatively participates in the work, and is in relation to therapist predominantly eagerly compliant. Usually patient begins the sessions by reporting his emotional condition and certain relevant events in his outside life and/or relationships, following which therapist makes a variety of interventions guided by his quest for "psychodynamic equations" (therapist's worksheet) with which to explain patient's symptoms, reactions, behavior. Patient clearly reveals his interest in the verbalized formulations that he received from therapist, usually listens intently and thoughtfully, often displays amazement at therapist's perspicacity, and expresses satisfaction or relief from the "insights." The work requests from therapist are mostly related to intellectual-cognitive activity consistent with his interest in "psychodynamic equations." The therapy is not explicitly structured around "the cardinal rule" of free association as the primary technique of communication. However, patient verbalizes readily and is encouraged by therapist from time to time to freely express his feelings and thoughts. In spite of this, patient does a good deal of suppressing.

From the beginning, patient tends to be compliantly accepting of therapist's confrontations, explanations, and interpretations, but at times he corrects misunderstandings or disagrees. On a number of occasions when therapist has forcefully and somewhat authoritatively attempted to pressure patient into accepting something with which he disagrees, or when therapist persists in expressing his ideas and does not permit patient the opportunity to express himself, patient assertively "fights for the floor." There are many such struggles of varying intensity in which patient tries, generally unsuccessfully, to get therapist to seriously consider his views. Usually patient gives in, and verbally accepts therapist's formulations. Feelings of disappointment, frustration, anger, hurt and sadness are observable in patient's behavior (tone of voice, facial expressions, etc.) but are rarely expressed verbally, patient becoming silent. This seems to be consistent with patient's character pattern of submissiveness to authority figures with partial inhibition of self-assertiveness. On a few notable occasions, patient manages to assert himself successfully and therapist modifies his interpretation in a manner more acceptable to patient, as in Session No. 5.

At the beginning of therapy, therapist stated in his work sheet that he felt respect for patient, then quickly developed a consciously depreciatory attitude toward him as he recognized patient's obvious passive-receptive, submissive masochistic character traits (therapist's work sheet).* In his primary focus upon psychodynamic formulations, therapist gave the impression often of not being aware of patient's immediate emotional reactions. As a result, he frequently appears unsympathetic and unempathic to patient's feelings. However, he often accompanies certain interventions with genial smiling and laughing as though to soften the possible narcissistic hurt. Therapist's depreciatory attitude, especially towards patient's masculinity, frequently reveals itself. At times, therapist's lack of empathy (therapist's work sheet) for patient's personality reveals itself overtly and patient shows his strongest reactions of

---

*Whenever "therapist's work sheet" is referred to in parentheses, the foregoing description is taken directly from therapist's own statements.

protest against the depreciation of his masculinity. Therapist frequently becomes pressuring, somewhat authoritative, at times moderately critical and/or scolding, particularly when his desire for patient to understand and accept his dynamic formulations is thwarted. For the most part, therapist has shown an actively interested, helping attitude, giving freely of his intellectual formulations. Therapist has been aware of patient's receptive strivings and that patient unconsciously takes in therapist's verbalizations as symbolic feedings (therapist's work sheet). Nevertheless, therapist is very active and thus generally gratifies patient's unconscious need to be "fed." At the same time, he is covertly and at times overtly critical of patient's receptive tendencies. Therapist states that he is deliberately not permitting patient to manipulate him into the "maternal" role. It seems probable, however, that therapist, by his own activity, and at times forcefulness unintentionally encourages and gratifies patient's dependent and submissive tendencies.

Therapist's technique consists, for the most part, of working out psychodynamic formulations based on his inferences from patient's behavior and verbal communications during sessions, and his intuitive understanding of the psychodynamic forces operating in the events and experiences that patient reports. To a lesser extent, therapist's formulations are based on direct verbalization by patient of some inner psychic experience (such as feeling afraid of retaliation, feeling guilty, feeling ashamed, etc.). Typically, therapist then presents his formulation to patient. If patient agrees intellectually, therapist frequently moves on to further intellectual work to obtain more clarification and understanding of the psychodynamic constellation. Patient's emotional reactions in the therapeutic interaction during the sessions are usually not focused on by either therapist or patient, although they are frequently observable by the team.

Patient usually is receptive to and thoughtful about therapist's confrontations and interpretations and attempts to confirm them if he can. For the most part, they deal with his relationships outside the therapy. Consequently, therapist and patient are usually attempting to identify and understand patient's reactions during some recent or remote experience prior to the session, resulting in a cognitive awareness that a given emotion existed and motivated a particular action or attitude.*

Therapist seems to wish for patient to recover his potency and to acquire understandings of the conflicts that, according to therapist's insights, empathy, and judgments, are significant dynamic factors in causing patient's neurotic symptoms and behavior patterns. Therapist also wants patient to become a more mature man with less receptive submissive tendencies and less hostility when these needs are thwarted. In addition, apparently he wishes patient to develop greater assertiveness, self-reliance, and generosity in his interpersonal relationships. However, therapist seems to require considerable compliance and submission toward himself and frequently seems to react negatively when patient does not conform to his wishes, and positively when he does. Therapist appears to have mixed feelings. He strives to give help to patient in a variety of ways, predominantly in achieving insights. He also gives what is essentially fatherly reassurance, advice, and guidance. His attitude is at times neutral, frequently warm and friendly, and, at times, depreciatory.

Patient reacts to therapist as though he were an omniscient, idealized parent whom he admires and respects greatly; with whom he eagerly and pleasurably participates in the work; with whose wishes he wants to comply; and from whom he enjoys receiving psychodynamic information, guidance, advice, and reassurance. Inferences from patient's behavior indicate a deeper wish for closeness, sympathy, acceptance, approval, and love, and an attempt to obtain these gratifications predominantly by means of compliance, submission, ingratiation, complaining, and the suppression and repression of aggression. Patient's assertiveness when occasionally overtly expressed toward therapist is generally not commented upon by therapist. However, there is no disapproval from therapist when patient asserts himself, and on a few occasions, does succeed in his self-assertive attempts toward therapist. It is inferred that a repressed fear of rejection by therapist is constantly operating and

---

*The following inferences about the emotional interaction between therapist and patient are made from observations by the team of the verbal and nonverbal behavior of the therapist and patient.

that it motivates patient to suppress most of his hurt, frustrated, or angry feelings in the interaction with therapist.

Therapeutic Experience of the Patient

Emotional Experience of Patient

Patient is obviously pleased and gratified to be treated by a therapist whom he respects, admires, and reveres, but he experiences and expresses anxiety lest he be rejected by therapist. In response to this, patient receives firm, warm reassurances from therapist about his acceptability, which apparently allays patient's immediate fear of rejection. Patient apparently wants to be accepted and liked by therapist, and to be a good and successful patient, and he attempted to achieve this by presenting a very informative anamnesis, during which he seemed to experience some catharsis of affect in relation to the precipitating events of his illness. Patient in the first two hours, apparently felt accepted by therapist.

Patient repeatedly represents himself to the therapist as someone whose potentials for happiness and gratification and dignity have been thwarted. He represents himself as a victim of unfair criticism, depreciation, and rejection by the significant figures of his life, and one upon whom excessive demands are made. In presenting himself to the therapist in this role and complaining about the significant figures in his life, he seems to arouse in the therapist contemptuous attitudes for his apparent inadequate masculinity. Presumably the patient hopes to evoke a sympathetic emotional response in the therapist. Instead of fulfilling patient's expectations, therapist makes vigorous, forceful, interpretations to the effect that patient does not wish to be a man and wishes to be a dependent child. The therapist becomes fairly aggressive and challenging when the patient resists these interpretations. Since patient is unaware of his passive-dependent longings, and pictures himself as being a thwarted and victimized but inherently adequate and mature person, he experiences these interpretations as a narcissistic injury (blow to his masculine pride) and experiences feelings of humiliation, frustration, and anger. On the other hand, patient frequently has the experience of feeling and believing that therapist is helping him. It is evident that, for the patient, this therapist is an idealized, omniscient, wise, helpful authority figure, and that patient's unconscious wishes for an ideal "good" parent are being gratified in fantasy.

Patient also derives much receptive-dependent gratification and probably enhancement of self-esteem from therapist's consistently interested and helpful attitude and activity, and apparently derives gratification from the therapist's intellectual "feeding." Also, there is gratification from the expectation that analysis with this therapist would greatly enhance his self-esteem. This gratification sometimes reaches ecstatic proportions when patient experiences therapist's communications as if they were magical revelations. It is also probable that patient feels helped because of the therapist's obvious underlying wish for the patient to be a mature, self-assertive, generous, aggressive, less inhibited, less guilt-ridden man. This probably implies to patient that therapist has confidence in patient's capacity to achieve these goals and therefore to be worthy of therapist's help. Having a respected and idealized masculine object for identification diminishes patient's anxiety and contributes to the patient's feelings of being helped. In certain areas of the reality, therapist treats patient with courtesy, consideration, and respect. The greetings and partings are accompanied by handshakes and generally suggest a sense of being welcomed by the therapist. The fees are arranged very much to the patient's satisfaction. The therapist displays his interest in the patient by working intensively and actively with the patient.

Patient has acquired some intellectual awareness of hypersensitivity to criticism from women, and of the concomitant reduction of self-esteem (hurt pride, shame, feelings of masculine inadequacy, feelings of inferiority). Patient has become more aware of his emotional patterns with his wife, especially his submissive and dependent attitudes, his inhibition of self-assertiveness and aggression, his failure to be adequately protective toward her, and the resultant feelings of guilt. He has learned to recognize that he feels resentment against his wife when she frustrates his narcissistic needs (to be admired, praised, succored), and that his resentment generates guilt feelings, since he does not rationally believe the resentment is justified. Patient has also developed increased awareness of his fear of rejection and being abandoned, his fear of anger from maternal figures, and fear of loss of maternal figures and the consequent inhibition of self-assertiveness due to guilt and a fear of punishment. As a result, he is submissive and compliant, which leads to further feelings of humiliation and lowered self-esteem, and at times an overcompensatory need to assert himself. The assumed relationship between these psychodynamics and the symptoms of impaired sexual functioning has been interpreted by therapist and to some degree intellectually accepted by patient, that is, that it is an expression of his resentment and retaliation against frustrating women expressed as a refusal to function as an adult male, and his unconscious wish to be a dependent child.

Also, patient becomes somewhat aware of his need for closeness, for love, especially in the family situation, and of his feelings of hostile envy toward his wife, whose family relationships are more satisfying than his. He becomes aware of the tendency to disregard his wife's dependent needs. He also relives and experiences hurt pride, sadness, and suppressed anger in remembering various episodes when his brother failed to reciprocate his love, although these feelings are not verbalized.

Patient seems to have developed some intellectual understanding that he feels inferior and inadequate because he himself is ashamed of and disapproves of his unconscious wish to be a little boy, to be dependent, to receive from and not give to women and that he feels guilty about his resentful feelings toward maternal figures when his dependent needs are not gratified, and when they want him to be a man.

Changes in Behavior and Symptoms

Patient reported increased sexual urges accompanied by increased self-esteem after the first week of therapy. He reports successful and gratifying intercourse between the eighth and ninth hours of therapy. He shows evidence of some increased ability to assert himself with his wife in a more realistic manner. The following hypotheses and inferences suggest themselves to explain the symptomatic improvements:

1. Patient has developed increased awareness of the connection

between hurt, angry feelings toward his wife and the loss of sexual urge and impotence. Reduced guilt over hostility and reduced fear of punishment (by rejection) leads to improved sexual function.

2. The expectation of cure and the fantasy gratification of passive dependent needs by this idealized, omnipotent therapist results in generalized reduction of anxiety, improved self-esteem, and improved ego function. Having a respected and idealized model for identification diminishes anxiety. The wish to please the idealized, strong, masculine, omnipotent therapist-parent figure and to earn his approval and respect and conform with therapist's values of masculinity leads to symptomatic improvement.

3. Some improvement of self-esteem and self-assertion may be due to a need to compensate for damaged self-esteem resulting from therapist's focusing on patient's receptive dependent submissive tendencies, similar to his mother's. Some improvement of self-assertiveness may be due to several corrective emotional experiences. The first occurred when patient does assertively protest (fifth hour), the therapist does not reject him and patient's expectations of punishment for self-assertion do not materialize. A similar extratherapeutic experience occurs when patient realistically refuses to submit to a demand of his wife, and discovers with surprise and relief that no retaliation occurred.

Therapist's View of the Observers Evaluations of the First Ten Sessions

There is no major discrepancy between therapist's and observers' *account of* events. The following mostly quantitative discrepancies in the *evaluations* are significant.

1. Therapist records his awareness in the second interview of a mild negative feeling toward the kind of conflict (demandingness toward wife and lack of generosity) patient displays. This is also recognized by the observers. Therapist and observers describe the patient's reaction to this negative feeling. The observers, however, overplay this negative feeling and are not sufficiently aware of the fact that already in the third interview therapist's growing intellectual and therapeutic interest is beginning to greatly overshadow the mild negative feelings. This is a quantitative difference between the

therapist's and observers' evaluation of the emotional interaction. The observers do not note that by the third interview the patient's confidence was substantially restored. The observers do not emphasize that this growing confidence, to a great degree, is due to the patient's feeling that therapist understands his problems and that his interpretations make sense. The observers exaggerate that the patient submissively accepts interpretations in order to be loved. They underrate the fact that at the same time the patient is rapidly gaining a genuine understanding. The observers most adequately list the different aspects of this insight and yet emphasize somewhat one-sidely the patient's need for love as the most *important motivating* factor. The discrepancy is a quantitative one. The therapist *gives more credit* to *patient's* genuine *insight* than the observers do.

2. The observers are obviously recognizing more acutely the inadvertent "disparaging" manifestation of therapist's negative feeling than the therapist is. Curiously, they do not recognize with equal sensitiveness the therapist's growing positive investment in the treatment and patient's grateful recognition of this warm feeling. They repeatedly mention that the patient got a great deal of gratification from the "intellectual food" he received yet do not give sufficient credit to this positive factor in explaining the fact, that after a half-year of complete impotence, the patient after the eighth interview regained his potency. All in all, the observers overstressed the therapist's "domination" and "pressuring," almost browbeating the patient, and yet admit that the therapist encourages the patient to express his hostile feelings (fourth and fifth interview). "I suppose they confuse therapist's emphatic statements and his urge to convey intellectual insight with aggressiveness and expression of negative feelings. I am convinced on the basis of careful introspection that this is a great overstatement." They repeatedly describe that therapist, by pointing out the patient's inability to act as an adult man toward his wife, humiliates the patient and pressures him to be a man. They forget that *the patient himself feels self-critical* but is not capable of fully recognizing what he dislikes in himself. It is not only the therapist's, but even more the patient's, desire to be a man. Bringing out the emotional reasons why the patient cannot live up to this ideal is

anything but humiliating. The therapist takes every opportunity to emphasize the extenuating circumstances, such as, for example, the family's attitude toward patient. In the fourth interview he intimates that probably brother was not stronger than patient. This is overlooked by the observers. Indeed, they omit to mention, that therapist uses every opportunity to show the patient that he is not as weak as he feels.

3. The observers do not recognize the ego-uplifting effect of therapist's pointing out that the patient distorts the therapeutic situation into a humiliating one following his internal need. The fact that in the fifth interview the patient is capable of expressing hostility shows that the interpretations and the basically positive attitude of the therapist decreases patient's fear of expressing himself freely. The dream about father's death reported in this hour confirms this evaluation.

There is a great deal of discrepancy between observers and therapist in the evaluation of the fifth interview. The observers emphasized again that the therapist's attitude is pressuring and critical and almost completely disregard that the atmosphere between patient and therapist is particularly warm and the therapist is supportive both in tone and behavior. It is a misinterpretation that the therapist "retreated" at the end of the interview when patient flared up because he misunderstood the therapist. Patient thought that the therapist said that he was not a man. The therapist, however, simply paraphrased what he thought the patient thought about himself. It was no retreat, but a correction of the patient's misinterpretation. The patient is only too ready to feel attacked. This is borne out from the whole content of this interview; its central topic is identification with the underdog. I cannot understand why the observers fell into the same misinterpretation as the patient except that they overidentified themselves with the patient and were sorry for him; together with the patient they rebelled against the authoritarian analyst. The therapist was eager to show the patient—both with his tone and voice and with the content of his interpretation—that the patient distorts the situation. If the observers have doubts about their error, I strongly suggest that the last part of this hour should be replayed and listened to. Without listening to it and reading only the words, such misinterpretation is easily understandable. This points to a possible source of error in the observers' procedure. It is obvious that the coordinator had the greatest influence in the formulations but he was the one who did not observe the interviews nor did he listen to the records. This could easily explain why his evaluations when the nonverbal elements were most significant are erroneous.

4. In the sixth interview the therapist reports some revival of his own negative reaction because of the patient's lack of generosity toward his wife. He recognizes that this came to expression in the bluntness of his interpretation of the patient's envy of his wife's getting support from his family. This demonstrates the fact that therapist is by now fully aware of his lack of sympathy with this specific trait of the patient. I believe that this enabled therapist to control to a great degree this feeling and prevent it from entering into the treatment situation to a disturbing degree. This was not difficult for him because of his growing positive feelings. I think the observers correctly are aware of the negative component but do not see how the positive feelings amply make up for the negative. If this were not true, the positive therapuetic response—return of potency—could not be easily accounted for.

5. There is a misstatement: "Therapist interprets patient's impotence as part of his general weakness." This is a misstatement. On the contrary, therapist explains this from a highly specific circumstance: the wife's increasing demandingness since she lost her own mother and then the substitute mother, that is to say, patient's mother. The patient does not agree "in a submissive fashion" but agrees because he becomes more and more aware that his impotence was a reaction to the increasing demands of wife and his losing maternal support. ("He and his wife are like two babes in the wood.")

6. The observers fail to see that in the seventh interview patient could make the confession that he overplays weakness and misery as an appeal for help. He could make this confession because he became more sure of the therapist's strong interest in him. He no longer needs this drastic measure to blackmail sympathy by being miserable. He feels he gets it anyway. The observers failed to understand this because they are still hipped to their original overemphasis, that the therapist is bulldozing the patient to accept

interpretations. They underestimate the fact that the interpretations are closely following the material and patient accepts them not only to please but also because he *feels* their relevance.

7. The greatest discrepancy is in the evaluation of the eighth interview, after which the patient became potent. The observers' description is a one-sided caricature of what really happened. They misinterpret the therapist's aim of giving a comprehensive view of the total situation as a kind of overactive assault not allowing the patient to express himself. Their description does not correspond to the therapist's acute subjective awareness that he gave his forceful explanation about patient's tendency to get sympathy by a show of weakness without having any negative feelings toward the patient. The tenor was to help patient by showing him his defenses and evasions. It is true that therapist made it clear that he has no sympathy with patient's display of weakness. This was, he felt, the best way to make patient conscious that he is not actually weak, but only play-acts weakness.

The observers missing this in the interview is not fully comprehensible to me. I advise that this hour should be played back and re-studied. The fact that after the interview, patient became potent speaks for the correctness of the evaluation of this interview. If the observers were right—namely, that the patient was crushed—this effect is not explainable.

In spite of these discrepancies, the therapist's and the observers' final evaluation of the ten sessions, particularly the reconstruction of the patient's emotional experiences and intellectual cognitive awareness, are basically similar. I believe that the main discrepancy comes from the observer's reaction to the therapist's style of treatment. I can only guess the reasons for some of their exaggerations in both description and evaluation.

A. They were unaccustomed to this type of active treatment, which is based on the principle of helping the patient's integrative functions by an immediate utilization of the spontaneously offered material; I mean, connecting immediately the material as much as it can be done, the patient's past and present experiences with his reactions to the therapist. This continuous integrative activity reduces resistance against unconscious material and makes possible a rather rapid flow of material that appears in a continuum. This technique is confused with aggressive pressuring although its effect is the opposite.

B. Possibly the observers caricatured therapist's style, as an opportunity to pass judgement on a senior colleague. Unconsciously, of course! This is, of course, only one of several factors.

C. I think the main reason for the observer's exaggerations is the fact that they, early in the treatment, discovered some latent negative transference and overcommitted themselves to this discovery. To remain consistent they harped on certain aspects of the interaction and neglected positive features which developed soon after the initial three interviews.

The other side of the medal: The observers more clearly recognized the therapist's idiosyncratic reactions and particularly their therapeutically unfavorable effects. They were less generous in recognizing the favorable effects of the therapist's personality features.

Conclusions

I believe that the main objective of this portion of our work— confrontation of the therapist's and observers evaluations—is to arrive at certain consistent characteristics of the two kinds of observations and evaluations. It would be beside the point to try to argue over who is right whenever there is disagreement. The position that the observers statements are "objective," while those of the therapist's subjective, is untenable. The observers are also subjective. The difference between them is the vantage point: participation versus nonparticipation.

About these ten interviews, I would make the following generalizations:

1. The observers report *is much richer in describing interaction.* The observers are in a better position to observe the patient's reaction to the therapist's interventions and attitudes. In the interpretation of therapist's reactions, however, they make errors (see eighth interview).

2. The observers account about the therapist's attitude and intentions is based on inferences; they by no means are factual statements. My conviction is that their account about the therapist is

richer in detail but often based on misinterpretations. In other words, their reconstruction of the therapist's emotional reactions is less reliable than the therapist's own introspective accounts. The latter, however, are less frequent; but whenever they are made are more accurate and reliable. This is natural of course. This advantage of the therapist's account does not exist if one tries to reconstruct the *therapist's unconscious attitudes, of course. Neither group can reliably reconstruct the therapist's unconscious motivation on the basis of the data available to them.*

3. The observers are more sensitive to those of therapist's activities that do not further the therapy. They are less generous in reporting the therapist's therapeutically favorable activities and attitudes. This is a natural outcome of the difference in vantage point; participation versus nonparticipation. Nevertheless, to be quite frank, I think that the observers did not give credit to the fact that the therapist was in continuous contact with the underlying dynamics, perhaps more than usual in an average treatment. Not that I want praise, but this continuous contact may be significant so far as the process is concerned. It may be responsible for the fact that within ninety-seven interviews the patient's basic conflicts were understood: his relation to mother, sister, father, and brother, as it determines his relations to professional colleagues; how these patterns contribute to his symptoms and determined the whole rhythm of his career (successes and failures). This factor (continued contact with dynamics) may have had a determining influence upon the changes in his marital and professional behavior. The report of the observers almost sounds as if the therapist's main influence was to pressure the patient into a passive obedience.

4. In the psychodynamic reconstruction of the process, there is a large degree of agreement between therapist and observers. Neither of them, however, seem to have a great advantage over the other. It may be stated that in general, because the observers are more preoccupied with the interaction, the therapist's psychodynamic reconstructions are richer and more cohesive. The reason for this is that the observers have the benefit of hearing much of the therapist's psychodynamic formulations when he transmits them to the patient. Probably, when they agree with these formulations,

and mostly they seem to agree, they do not bother to repeat them in detail in their account.

4. To be as objective as possible, the therapist is ready to admit that he is somewhat defensive when his therapeutic behavior and style is described. He feels this defensiveness and wants to report it as an empirical fact. Whether he is defensive because his narcissism is hurt or because his activities are sometimes misunderstood is difficult to establish. It is, however, *highly* probable that both factors play a role.

In order to make this processing constructive, the same degree of objectivity should be required from the observers. They should consider particularly the previously listed points:

1. that they committed themselves to their early recognition of certain countertransference reactions and to remain consistent overemphasized these observations and continued to emphasize them and become less sensitive to the changes in therapist's attitude;

2. that they were unaccustomed to therapist's style and did not fully recognize its advantages and mainly saw its disadvantages (they equated activity with pressuring);

3. that they (unconsciously) utilized this experiment to pass judgement on a senior colleague.

Final Remarks

For our project the following generalizations seem to be of primary importance. In spite of quantitative differences in the observers' and therapists' evaluation of the process, the following can be stated:

1. The therapist's personality, that is, his values, have a strong influence on the specific nature of the therapuetic interaction. In this special case the therapist's idea, how a man should treat his wife, obviously colored his interventions. Another man, for example, whose image of husband-wife interrelation is more a 50-50 proposition, would have more sympathy with the patient's expectations from his wife. This would have differently influenced the course of the treatment. Whether this is good or bad for the therapy is a difficult question to decide. My stand in this question is well-

known; if the therapist's value-attitudes are different from those of the persons who played a decisive role in the patient's development, this is favorable for the treatment. In this special case, patient's father's marital orientation and particularly his attitude toward his children seems to be radically different from that of the therapist.

2. The general interpersonal climate in this case was at least as effective in influencing the therapeutic process as cognitive insight arrived at by intellectual formulations and interpretations. This could be only demonstrated by a special detailed study.

3. Corrective emotional experiences as noted by the observers and occasionally by the therapist have a definite effect in bringing about changes in patient's reactions. The one example quoted by the observers was therapist's tolerance toward patient's open expression of resentment, which was in contrast with mother's attitude. This seemed to help the patient to behave more self-assertively. The therapist's intensiveness and eagerness to explain to patient the dynamics of his reactions may also be in sharp contrast to father's lack of interest in patient. Also, mother's attitude was different from that of the therapist. She was aggressive but certainly did not try to explain and to teach patient but to use him for her emotional needs. It is probable that this "intellectual feeding" with a strong emphasis on helping patient was the main dynamic factor in patient's overcoming his complete impotence of many months duration. This type of generous "feeding" is in sharp contrast to the demandingness of the mother. The patient's objection to accepting the role of a husband toward his wife diminished because he received a great deal of gratification from this intellectual feeding. This certainly contributed to his regaining his potency. To quantitatively compare the effect of this emotional factor with that of cognitive insight is not possible since both factors were present simultaneously.

Comparison between Observers and Therapist

In the interpersonal experience, the team and therapist agree that therapist's active interest in the work is experienced by patient as an interest in him and functions positively to increase patient's feelings of acceptance and worthiness. Therapist and team are not in accord about the quantitative amount of patient's unexpressed desire for therapist's approval, regard, and love and the degree to which he uses the device of compliance in the hope of satisfying these desires. The team and therapist are in agreement that shame connected with passive-dependent wishes is of crucial importance in this patient's character structure. However, the team considers that the therapist's nonverbally communicated dissatisfaction with the patient's passive-dependent tendencies affected the patient's self-esteem. In an attempt to counteract the heightened shame, and in an attempt to receive the therapist's approval, regard, and respect, he unconsciously complies with what he considers to be the therapist's wishes and standards, which are to some extent also his own.

Similarly, the team regards some of patient's agreements with therapist's formulations as intellectual and motivated by wishes to comply and please, while therapist regards them as true insights. There are many points of agreement between team and therapist about patient's new awarenesses. The team considers guilt about aggression and fear of punishment in the form of rejection as dynamically more operative than the therapist does. Accordingly, the team regards the reduction in guilt and fear associated with self-assertion and hostility as crucial factors in the return of potency and the increase in self-assertion. Therapist and team regard the experience with therapist in this regard as a corrective emotional experience. Both team and therapist believe that as patient developed more insight into connecting low self-esteem and his passive-dependent tendencies, it became an important force in motivating him toward increased self-assertion and independence. Team and therapist agree tht therapist's values play a significant role. However, the team attributes importance to patient's unconscious desire to comply with therapist's values and the unconscious striving to identify with therapist as a masculine ideal.

In summary, the team makes more observations about the interpersonal interactional process. Based on these observations the team ascribes greater importance to the effect of the therapist's personality (his behavior and attitudes) than does the therapist. The team makes more observations about the patient's intrapersonal (intrapsychic) processes, but does not attribute as much importance to them in the changes observed in the patient as therapist does. This is apparently due to the fact that the therapist focuses predominantly on the patient's psychodynamic processes as he conceptualizes them from the patient's verbal productions, and focuses much less on the patient's reactions in the interpersonal interactions during the sessions than does the team.

Unfortunately, we have the therapist's review of the observers' comments only for the first ten sessions because the therapist died before the process of all our data was completed. The therapist's data about the entire project was available and was used by the observers to complete the project. However, the therapist's comments about the observers' views of the first ten sessions clearly demonstrate the agreements and disagreements that can occur between the therapist and observers. It should be noted that page 51 to page 59, dealing with the therapist's reactions to the observers' comments, are in the therapist's own words.

7

Therapy—Sessions 11–21

Summary of Manifest Events

Session No. 11 (13 February 1958)

Patient and therapist interchange ideas about patient's lack of self-esteem and inordinate need for prestige in his work. Patient stresses his sensitivity to criticism, and therapist states that patient's pride interferes with his teaching. He offers himself as a model of a good teacher. When patient attempts to connect his hypersensitivity with his ungratified longing for love from mother and brother, therapist, in an active and forceful manner, confronts patient with his own dynamic formulations of his behavior. Patient reacts by agreeing verbally with these formulations but reveals nonverbally feelings of sadness and anger.

Session No. 12 (17 February 1958)

The hour centers on patient's hostility to mother and rivalry toward siblings. Therapist reassures patient when the latter voices suspicion that therapist may fail to protect his anonymity. He explains patient's distrust as a displacement to therapist of his hostility toward mother and brother. When therapist's speculation about patient's triumphing over brother because of his getting therapy is factually disproven by patient, therapist admits error but insists that patient has a need to provoke brother. The hour ends in disagreement as therapist confronts patient with having negative feelings and patient denies this.

Session No. 13 (20 February 1958)

Patient, after mentioning that he has had successful intercourse, describes his depressive feelings when he identified with mentally ill people. Therapist interprets patient's need for suffering in the martyr role, stressing his submission to brother. Patient disagrees, but praises therapist by labeling him a good, giving parent figure. After considerable blocking, he stresses at length his anger toward Dr. S. but he again reaches out to therapist by praising him, apparently wanting therapist's reassurance. He finally sadly and compliantly agrees with therapist that he has a tendency to trip himself up.

Session No. 14 (24 February 1958)

The discussion between patient and therapist concerns patient's fear of being rejected for being aggressive and therapist's reassurance that he is accepted. There is some lightness as therapist laughs and patient joins in. Patient blocks and becomes irritable when therapist points out to him his dramatization of the martyr role but finally accepts this interpretation. Patient then talks about the weekend and his children and expresses dissatisfaction with his own functioning as a father. Therapist is empathic and reassuring to patient.

Session No. 15 (27 February 1958)

Patient talks about his children and is critical of his younger son. He relates a dream in which he is a child and having intercourse with his sister and stopping for fear of injuring her. This is analyzed and therapist, in a gentle fashion, points out patient's sibling rivalry with sister. Therapist connects this with patient's identifying sister with his younger son. Therapist is reassuring as he tells patient about the universality of childhood residues. He stresses patient's aggressive resentment to women using the content of the dream. Patient enters into the work actively in an animated fashion when therapist urges him to go further and analyze his hostility in sex. Patient complies and states that before his impotence, he had an increase in his sexual drives.

Session No. 16 (3 March 1958)

After some friendly banter initiated by patient and participated in by therapist, the hour centers on patient's explaining his fear of giving up his dependent role and assuming a masculine one. He resents therapist's labeling his remarks as intellectualizing. Therapist's direct question about sex leads to a discussion about it with therapist enlightening patient about the desirability of spontaneity in sex. Patient discloses the connection between his impotence and his fear of responsibility. The rest of the time is devoted to discussion of his sister's visit and patient's comparing her with wife. He stresses his preference of wife's qualities.

Session No. 17 (6 March 1958)

After venting his anger at therapist's indifferent way of notifying him at the end of the previous hour about the forthcoming interruption, patient continues during most of the hour to confront therapist with his lack of empathy and sympathy for his dependent needs. Therapist at times defends himself directly by saying that the interruption will be productive for patient, and by interpreting the dynamics of patient's symptoms, stresses patient's dependency role. Patient is determined to put across his point and emphasizes that while he is stronger than when he started treatment, he is not yet well enough to be left without preparation. He talks about Dr. S., his previous therapist, having let him down when he needed him most, implying that therapist does the same. Patient persists in expressing his dissatisfaction and therapist admits that he has not realized the intensity of patient's feelings. Patient is now content and therapist warmly shakes patient's hand.

Session No. 18 (10 March 1958)

The session revolves about patient's sibling rivalry; he stresses that his exaggerated need for love is based on having unsuccessfully reached out to parents and brother and having been rejected by them. When, after admitting shamefacedly, that he pried into brother's analysis by asking what role he played in it, patient says that he wished brother to suffer as he did. Then he describes his sadness because his feeling toward his younger son is not sufficiently tender. To the surprise of therapist, patient bursts into tears when therapist interprets that patient identifies his younger son with brother. Therapist, attempting to decrease patient's tension, focuses on relieving his guilt and points out that his hostility is a reaction to not getting love. Throughout the hour, therapist is friendly and very empathic and reassuring after patient's weeping outburst. He ends the session on a light note with patient gratefully entering into it.

Session No. 19 (13 March 1958)

Patient complains, in whining manner most of the session, that he does not get enough from his wife and children. Patient describes that his attempt at sex the night before was unsatisfactory, and insists that he is in need at the present time of dependent gratification. He talks about separation anxiety, about which he read, and ignores most of therapist's interpretations about his excessive wishes to receive; thereupon therapist seems annoyed and stresses patient's hostility, possessiveness, clinging, and concentration on infantile traumatic experiences and finally tells him directly to give up the "claim check" to dependency as it cannot be gratified now by anyone, including the therapist. Therapist also tells patient that if he gives up his infantile functioning and assumes an adult role, he will function adequately sexually. The hour seems to represent a naughty complaining boy with a strong, realistic parent who tells him the facts of life.

Session No. 20 (17 March 1958)

The session centers on therapist's stressing patient's dependent needs, his inability to share, his possessiveness, and his hostility.

The impending interruption is discussed. Both therapist and patient work actively in their attempt to increase patient's intellectual insight before treatment is interrupted. The discussion revolves about patient's exaggeration of his dependence, his resentment of the realistic dependent needs of others, and his fear of responsibility. Therapist interprets the displacement of his hostility from mother to wife and from brother to younger son. Patient associates to this by relating his anger toward Dr. S., apparently displacing his anger from therapist to Dr. S. Patient guards against disclosing his real affect or exposing new material in this hour in view of this being almost the last session for a while.

Therapist's goal seems to be to give patient sufficient insight and encouragement to tide him over the therapeutic interruption.

Session No. 21 (18 March 1958)

Discussion centers around patient's reactions to the impending interruption, his fear of displeasing and losing love objects, his need for reassurance, and his dependency. The important event in the interpersonal interaction is therapist's reassuring attitude and patient's crying when therapist expresses confidence in patient's ability to handle his problems.

Therapist-Patient Interaction

The interpersonal relationship during these sessions remains essentially the same as during the first ten hours, except that therapist focuses more on patient's feelings. On the whole, therapist continues to be quite active, at times forceful and pressuring, at times guiding and directive, and at times kindly and empathic. Patient continues to cooperate, on the whole willingly and compliantly, in the work.

The transference neurosis has become clearer, and consists primarily of patient fantasizing therapist as an idealized parent, predominantly mother, who is strong, omniscient, giving, and from whom he is constantly but largely unconsciously attempting to get approval, sympathy, empathic understanding (sign of love) and toward whom he consciously feels warmth, admiration, and gratitude. Nonverbal behavior indicates that tender feelings are present. Two members of the team infer that some unconscious erotic feelings are also present. Frequently the desires for gratification are thwarted because it appears that the therapist primarily concerns himself with the intellectual work. At times he seems not very empathic and becomes critical, or annoyed, especially when patient's wishes and demands for gratification become overt and directed toward him. Patient's reactions of hurt, sad, angry feelings are usually suppressed, not focused on, and covered over by his positive feelings toward therapist as the idealized parent. Patient usually manages to avoid focusing on the experiences with therapist and despite the frustrations, generally manages to end each session with feelings of satisfaction and warm mutuality with therapist. This is accomplished by patient complying with therapist's wishes regarding the work, agreeing with and confirming therapist's formulations if he possibly can, and thus finishing the session with the satisfying feeling of having received "good things" from the therapist, and being pleased with himself for having "learned" something, probably preconsciously experiencing, as a result, the closeness and "being loved" that he intensely craves. Some gratification of submissive masochistic strivings are at times unconsciously experienced.

During the seventeenth and eighteenth hours patient struggles with some success to get more empathic reactions from therapist. He asserts himself about therapist's lack of appreciation of the intensity of his feelings about the interruption, following which therapist becomes much more kindly, empathic, and, at times, tender. In the eighteenth hour intense affect in the form of crying breaks through. It is probably connected with deep feelings of grief due to recent and old rejections by his brother, mobilized by the sudden, unexpected gratification of his hitherto suppressed and frustrated longings for tenderness and love from therapist. Guilt feelings connected with hostility to his son and his brother probably also contributed to the crying. It is probable that therapist unconsciously reacts to patient's overtly expressed disappointment in therapist's lack of perceptiveness and responsiveness in the sixteenth and seventeenth hours, and unconsciously makes amends. This is followed in the nineteenth hour by therapist again withdraw-

ing his tenderness and empathy, and becoming once again a somewhat pressuring, demanding, somewhat critical parent substitute,
who directs patient to renounce his strivings for dependent gratifications. Therapist consciously is motivated by his desire to have
patient give up his infantile demands for realistic therapeutic reasons. Patient's reaction, which is revealed in the twentieth hour, is
to repress these dependent strivings. He succeeds in complying
with therapist's unverbalized wish that he not have intense infantile
longings and focuses his attention instead on his mature resources,
capabilities, and strivings, and accepts therapist's statement that
the interruption is good for him. The feelings of rejection and anger
appear subsequently displaced onto his former therapist. Following
this, therapist behaves in an amiable, empathic manner, revealing
that he is pleased. The inference is made that therapist is pleased
with patient's compliance with his unverbalized wishes (that patient
not be disturbed by the interruption and that he renounce his
"demandingness").

In the twenty-first hour an intensely emotional experience in the
interpersonal relationship occurs. While discussing patient's past
emotional deprivations with his mother and brother, therapist is
unusually warm and kindly and explicitly verbalizes confidence in
patient's ability to solve his problems. Patient cries at this point,
indicating an intense emotional response to therapist's expression
of a positive attitude toward him, something that he does not
expect. Therapist describes in his worksheet that he has "feelings
of satisfaction" with the "analytic work" and that patient "is
taking the interruption well." The assumption can be made that
therapist's more than usual positive attitude toward patient is a
result of these feelings of satisfaction with patient's compliance in
renouncing his "dependency claim check," as well as a response
to patient's need for emotional gratification. Therapist states in his
worksheet that he is deliberately creating a "corrective emotional
experience" by expressing "trust" in contrast to the mother's
"distrust." The assumption is made that patient's deep feelings of
pleasure and relief connected with feeling valued and "loved" by
an important parent-surrogate after a long period of emotional
starvation are so intense that discharge in crying occurs. Subsequently, therapist expresses additional positive attitudes toward

patient by explicitly reassuring him that he has proven he is a man and that it is not necessary for him to prove it by means of sex with his wife. It is probable that this experience, in which patient received signs of esteem from an important parental surrogate, constitutes a corrective emotional experience in view of the blows to his self-esteem connected with depreciation from his mother. It is important to note that therapist (parent surrogate) indicates that he accepts patient as a man and that he considers him capable of functioning as one and capable of renouncing his "dependency." It can be assumed that this is gratifying to patient and that it will help in enhancing his self-esteem, and will increase his strivings toward the adult masculine role and repression of his dependent strivings.

Therapeutic Experience of the Patient

In the Interpersonal Relationship with Therapist

Although for the most part patient continues to experience therapist as a relatively forceful and pressuring parent-surrogate during these hours, a number of significant differences are beginning to make their appearances. Therapist is gradually becoming less depreciatory, and in the therapist-patient interaction tends to be generally kinder to patient, particularly when patient is compliantly cooperative in the cognitive intellectual work, or seems to be showing signs of progress. At one point, in the eighteenth session, when patient reacts with extremely intense emotion to an interpretation made by therapist, therapist responds with a degree of gentleness and tenderness that he had never before shown to patient. On the other hand, in the very next session, when patient again becomes passively demanding, therapist reacts with his previous irritation and forceful pressures on patient to renounce his "claim check." Again, however, patient compliantly improves in the following (twentieth) session, and therapist responds by once more becoming amiable and empathic. Therapist overtly expresses confidence for the first time, in Session No. 21, that patient will be able to solve his problems, bringing "tears of joy" to patient's eyes and moving him deeply.

It may be inferred, therefore, that in the interpersonal relationship, patient experiences therapist as an interested, forceful, and pressuring parent-surrogate who rewards compliance with his standards of improved, mature behavior with acceptance and approval (therapist at one point—Session No. 11—overtly offers himself as a model for mature behavior), and responds to passive-demanding behavior by depreciation and withdrawal of approval. Therapist's casual announcement at the end of the sixteenth session of an impending therapeutic interruption, and his sarcastically jocular dismissal of patient's histrionic despair about it in the seventeenth session, is an example in point which may have constituted a kind of "corrective emotional experience" for patient of his "claim-check" pattern (one member of the team does not regard this as a corrective emotional experience, but considers that therapist's attitude merely fosters repression of patient's emotional reactions and needs). In addition, patient characteristically complies by repressing his feelings about the interruption.

In Session No. 21 patient has a deeply moving and gratifying experience when therapist expresses trust and confidence in patient's ability to solve his problems. The feeling is equated by patient with the "warm" feelings that he experienced with his wife at the beginning of his marriage, and warrants the inference that at this point patient feels that therapist values and cares for him. This event in the twenty-first session is probably a significant corrective emotional experience for patient in view of his lifelong feelings of rejection and depreciation by his parents and siblings.

New or Increased Awarenesses

A. In the course of these hours, patient acquired an increased awareness, primarily at a cognitive-intellectual level, of the following:
1. His need for prestige; and his hurt pride and hostility when his need is thwarted.
2. His masochistic need to suffer and its possible relationship to guilt over aggression; also of his apparent masochistic tendency to provoke people.
3. His submissive relationship to his brother.

4. His "demandingness" and desire for attention and gratification from significant love-objects in his life—particularly mother, brother, wife and therapist.
5. His sibling rivalry feelings, and their displacement on to
his children, particularly his younger son.
6. His wish to be the sole possessor of the love-object and
its possible association with feelings of deprivation at
having had to share his mother with his brother.
7. His resentment at the responsibilities of being a father
and a husband, and at the demands that these roles make
on him which he experiences as burdensome.
8. His warm and erotic feelings toward his sister, together
with resentment at her favored relationship to mother.
9. His mother's "hostile nature" and his resentment of it;
and recognition that his fear of rejection is related to his
lifelong fear of displeasing mother.
10. The relationship between his anger at his wife and his
impotence.

B. In addition, patient experienced at an emotional level, the
following:
1. Fear of rejection as retaliation for self-assertiveness or
for displeasing love-objects, and probable additional corrective emotional experiences as he discovered that the
feared retaliation (punishment) did not occur as expected.
2. Greater awareness of positive feelings toward therapy
and therapist, and of his desires for genuine feelings and
interest from therapist.

*The Following Symptomatic or Behavioral Changes Seem to Be
Occurring during This Period*

A. Patient's behavior to therapist is beginning to become somewhat less obviously boyish, ingratiating, and compliant.
B. He is developing a greater detachment in his relationship with
his mother, and experiences less narcissistic hurt when criticized
or slighted by her.

C. His impotence is improved, although still partially present.

Comparison between Observers and Therapist

Therapist and team are generally in agreement about the content of patient's cognitive-intellectual insights. The team differs from the therapist in identifying increased conscious awareness of several emotional experiences as described above.

In the descriptions of the interpersonal interactions, the team makes many more detailed observations and inferences than the therapist does, based on their much greater focusing on both therapist's and patient's behavior during the sessions. In this block of sessions, therapist is in greater agreement with the team than formerly in regard to patient's wish to please, but the team again puts greater emphasis on patient's compliance and desire for affection and approval as he reacts to therapist's actions and reactions, that is, on the actual relationship. The team considers many more of therapist's actions as due to unconscious reactions to patient than does therapist, especially in respect to patient's attitudes and behavior relevant to the passive demanding versus the independent adult patterns.

The team and the therapist have different hypotheses about the dynamics of the crying episodes, but no validation is possible because of insufficient exploration. The team and the therapist are in agreement that therapist's expressing trust and confidence in patient's ability to solve his problems results in patient's feeling valued and unconsciously loved in contrast to his customary feelings of rejection and depreciation with his parents and siblings. The team, accepting therapist's statement in his worksheet about his conscious motivation, differ from therapist in their inference of deeper motivations connected with therapist's conscious satisfaction that patient was reacting to the interruptions in the way therapist wanted, that is, "taking the interruption well." The therapist advances the hypothesis that patient identifies with therapist (by giving correct formulations) "in order to diminish the trauma of the interruption." The team, on the basis of its observations, describe patient's suppression of many of his feelings connected with the interruption and the separation, and attribute patient's "taking the interruption well" to his compliance with therapist's obvious wish for him to take it well. The team also attributes patient's "acting like a man" about it to a similar nonconscious motivation to comply and attempt to please therapist in order to retain therapist's approval and regard.

8

Therapy—Sessions 22–28

Summary of Manifest Events

Session No. 22 (10 April 1958)

Patient disappointed because he arrived three days before scheduled session and didn't find therapist, and in addition, on being told by therapist of another forthcoming interruption, he reacts by sighing and looking sad. He blames his insecurity on the responsibilities of marriage and parenthood. He reports improvement in sexual function, but adds that he has a fear of losing his wife if he does not satisfy her. Therapist, in an objective manner, interprets patient's impotence as a rejection of the masculine role and confronts him with the secondary gain from the illness. Generally, it can be stated that therapist sets the session on a cognitive-intellectual level and patient follows suit.

Session No. 23 (14 April 1958)

Both therapist and patient struggle during the beginning of the session, therapist with his irritation because he had car trouble that made him late and patient with annoyance at the delay. Patient complains about being depreciated by brother and brother surrogate and about his inadequate sexual drive. He reports that he turned down his wife's sexual invitation, something he never did before. Therapist emphasizes patient's passive, dependent needs. Despite this, patient, in a naive, nagging, passive and dependent manner asks repeatedly for guidance. Therapist refuses these requests, explains that he can only give him insight and focuses on patient's deficient generosity in the sexual field. Patient gratefully states that the therapist put him on the right track.

Session No. 24 (17 April 1958)

The session concerns itself with patient's pleading for more support from therapist and therapist pointing out to him that his bid for dependence and regression is unnecessary and that all that he can give him is insight. Therapist confronts patient with the ambivalence consisting of his wishing to get well and yet to remain in therapy for a long time. He ties this to patient's dependence on mother and his resentment at wife for having forced him to side with her against mother. Therapist suddenly turns the attention away from patient's feelings about his mother by asking directly "How are things going at home?" Patient admits that his reaction to his wife is changing. Toward the end of the session when patient asks for a sedative, therapist refuses. Patient shows no reaction to the refusal.

Session No. 25 (24 April 1958)

Patient complains because therapist missed the last appointment. Therapist offers an explanation and suggests that the impending interruption will be beneficial. Patient talks of his sexual difficulties and therapist is supportive, comforting, and reassuring. Patient complains that he was refused a loan by his brother-in-law. Therapist confronts him with his dependent and receptive needs. Patient then complains that his anonymity is not sufficiently protected and receives assurance.

Session No. 26 (28 April 1958)

When patient, admitting dependence on therapist, voices his resentment about the forthcoming long vacation, therapist confronts him wtih his overevaluation of the time element in treatment. Patient, after defending himself by pointing out the inordinate length of the vacation, speculates that it may be due to the fact that the observing team will be away and pleads with therapist to see him anyway. Therapist, after pointing out patient's need to be treated with special attention, states that this cannot be. Patient compliantly voices his understanding of the problem. He then reports successful intercourse and boldly speculates that he may have transferred anger from wife to therapist and, therefore, can be tender to wife. Both therapist and patient agree on the advisability of patient's giving up the infantile dependent state, whereupon therapist offers patient a cigarette, which patient accepts. The discussion shifts to a comparison of patient's feeling toward wife and sister.

Session No. 27 (1 May 1958)

Patient expresses fear of losing valuable items. Therapist interprets this as being due to his pressure on patient to give up his "wanting" attitudes. In a friendly and supportive fashion, he urges patient to give up his dependent longings. Patient verbally accepts this, but sighs and appears unhappy. Therapist reassures him that he will not be forsaken as long as he needs treatment. Patient perks up and compliantly corroborates therapist's implication that he wishes for rather than needs dependency. Therapist, gratified, states that he and patient are allies and partners in the treatment and urges patient to search for the dynamics of his problems. Patient complies and spends the rest of the hour talking about his sister and mother and doesn't show any obvious reaction when the session is interrupted after only thirty-one minutes.

Session No. 28 (5 May 1958)

Patient attempts to get sympathy from therapist by voicing various complaints. Therapist is reassuring and patient claims that he is satisfied and shifts to intellectualizing about his conflict in accepting the adult role. Both therapist and patient enter into a discussion about anger, therapist urging patient to express it. Patient in the attempt to please therapist is enthusiastic about his improvement. Patient veers away in a new direction—his relationship with his sister and his rivalry with her. Therapist takes over with a complicated theoretical formulation about patient's emotional involvement with members of his family. Patient apparently overwhelmed, compliantly agrees with therapist, stressing how interesting it is and ends the session with good wishes for therapist's vacation.

Therapist-Patient Interaction

On resumption of therapy after therapist's ten-day absence, the therapist-patient interaction is essentially unchanged. Patient continues in his attempts to insure therapist's acceptance and approval and to deal with his fear of rejection by "not having intense feelings about the interruption"; by suppressing his reactions of frustration, sadness, and anger about the interruptions and therapist's absence on Monday; and by cooperatively participating in the cognitive-intellectual discussions. He continues to try to manipulate therapist into the giving, omniscient, "magical" parental role by asking for reassurances, by complaining, and by praising and flattering therapist. Therapist is aware of patient's demands on him and conveys his wish for patient to give up his demanding attitudes. On the one hand he frustrates patient's dependency wishes by his attitudes about the interruptions of the therapy, his refusal to give him medication, and his refusal to see him without the team of observers. On the other hand, despite some mild irritation, therapist gratifies patient's receptive dependent wishes through his own activity, frequent interpretations, explanations, and active directing. Thus a struggle seems to be going on between therapist and patient in which patient agrees with therapist that he should give up the child role and his receptive wishes, but continues to attempt to manipulate therapist into gratifying his wishes by means of compliance, ingratiation, and complaining, and by suppressing his frustrations and resentments in relation to therapist. Therapist clearly communicates his desire for patient to mature.

In Session No. 24 therapist's elaborate justifications and explanations about interruptions and cancellations suggest some conflict about his handling of these matters, presumably connected with some negative feelings toward patient and his wish to "get the treatment over as quickly as possible" (therapist's work sheet).

Therapist's manner is on the whole objective, kindly, and friendly. He persists in his attempt to influence patient to renounce his "passive-dependent demands" and his regressive tendencies. At one point in the twenty-sixth session he spontaneously offers patient a cigarette and states in his work sheet that he does this "deliberately to ease patient's dependent needs." In line with his desire for patient to renounce his wish for gratification from therapist as a parent, therapist, in the twenty-seventh session, invites and encourages patient to be more his equal, to be a partner who will carry his responsibility in the work. Thus he encourages patient's mature strivings and invites his identification with therapist and discourages and covertly prohibits the "infantile" tendencies. Therapist tempers his demand however with reassurances that patient will continue to receive what he needs and that therapist does not expect him to give up his dependent patterns more rapidly than is feasible. In the twenty-eighth session, the last session before another interruption, patient succeeds in "seducing" therapist into giving him considerable gratification through reassurances and explanations despite therapist's warnings that he should not expect much "dependent" gratification. From therapist's work sheet, it is clear that therapist now recognizes patient's technique of compliance and his technique of confirming therapist's interpretations and is aware of the amount of gratification that patient obtains in the intellectual work, from therapist's psychodynamic explanations, and from the receiving of "insights." Despite therapist's encouraging patient to express the anger he feels toward therapist, patient manages to suppress his negative feelings about therapist's leaving, thus avoiding his fear of rejection and maintaining the satisfying harmony with the "good" parental figure.

Therapeutic Experience of Patient

In the Interpersonal Relationship with Therapist

Except for occasional brief lapses into irritability, therapist's behavior to patient during this period continues to be generally kindly, accepting, and friendly. Patient continues to experience therapist's approval for being cooperative in the cognitive-intellectual work of the therapy, and also for apparently renouncing his dependent-receptive wishes in relation to therapist, accepting the interruptions of the therapy, and "giving up" his negative reactions. At the same time, patient receives much gratification from therapist's active verbalization, as well as from therapist's reassurances that patient can be an "adult." In Session No. 26, patient is able to verbalize anger over therapist's long summer vacation without experiencing any retaliation from therapist. In Session No. 26 and No. 27, therapist's refusal to give patient "special treatment," and his structuring of the treatment as a "partnership" in which patient must play the active role and therapist merely the part of "helper," assists patient in identifying with therapist's patterns of maturity and puts pressure on patient to give up the child role in relation to therapist.

In general during this period, patient continues to get acceptance from therapist by complying with therapist's wishes—by acquiring and exhibiting intellectual insights and behavioral improvements, and by concealing, for the most part, his frustrations and resentments in relation to therapist. It is possible also that some incorporation of therapist's standards and values regarding maturity is beginning to take place. During this period therapist actively fosters the working alliance and the patient seems to cooperate in the therapeutic work.

New or Increased Awarenesses

During this period patient acquired an increased awareness of the following:
1. His fear of losing love objects (especially his wife and therapist).
2. His feelings of insecurity, and needs for reassurance, for parental "love" and care from his wife, his brother, his mother, and therapist.
3. His tendency to regress to the dependent role whenever the opportunity presents itself.

4. His positive tender and erotic, as well as hostile and competitive feelings toward his sister; his identification of sister and mother with each other; and his wish to "fuse" his sister and wife.

Symptomatic or Behavioral Changes
   1. Indications of increasing independence and self-reliance.
   2. Gradual emergence of more mature attitudes to therapist.
   3. Improving sexual relationship with wife.

Comparison between Observers and Therapist

Therapist and team are in agreement about the following increased awareness by patient:

1. His need for emotional support; love; care from wife, brother, mother, and therapist. The team is more specific in describing these needs, while therapist calls them "dependency."
2. The ambivalence toward sister and the identification of sister, mother, and wife.

Therapist describes many other insights of patient's that team does not regard as insights, but appraise as therapist's psychodynamic formulations with which patient tends to give verbal agreement or compliant superficial acceptance.

Team observes that patient is developing some increased awareness of (1) his fear of losing love objects, especially wife and therapist; (2) his tendency to regress to the dependent role when he gets the opportunity. These are not stressed by therapist.

In the interpersonal interaction, team and therapist are fundamentally in agreement about patient's attempt to get receptive gratification from therapist, therapist's frustration of these attempts, and therapist's overtly expressed desire for, and encouragement of, patient to give up his receptive strivings and be a more mature adult. The team makes more observations than therapist about patient's unexpressed reactions to his frustrations with therapist. The team also describes more receptive gratification for patient as a result of therapist's considerable cognitive-intellectual activity than does therapist, although therapist explicitly identifies patient's cooperating in this intellectual activity in order not to alienate therapist. The difference lies in the quantitative emphasis that team places on patient's attempt to please therapist. The team also emphasizes patient's reactions to the interruptions more than does therapist, and especially that he is able to express some resentment and that no retaliation ensues. The team emphasizes the fear of loss of love and approval as a motive for the inhibition of aggression and the submissive attitudes more than does therapist, who seems to regard the submissive attitude more as a defense against hostility, that is, a predominantly intrapersonal process. The team emphasizes more that the therapist's overtly expressed demand for patient to give up his receptive wishes makes it necessary for this patient, with his fear of loss of approval and love, to utilize suppression and to behave more independently and maturely.

9

Therapy—Sessions 29–47

Summary of Manifest Events

Session No. 29 (15 May 1958)

This was the first session after ten days' interruption. Therapist and patient seem to be in a struggle in which patient, although admitting improvement, tries to minimize it by complaining about symptoms and therapist confronts patient with his complaining and demanding attitudes. Therapist urges patient to give up his dependent demands, and patient manipulates the situation in the hope of receiving from therapist what he wanted as a child from his parents. In the attempt to get sympathy from therapist, patient complains bitterly that parents favored the sister and brother in preference to himself. There is an intellectual interchange about the competitive feeling that patient has toward his brother and other men, which is concealed by his passive-submissive reactions. The session ends with patient's admitting his increased independence and self-assertion.

Session No. 30 (20 May 1958)

Patient, tense and somewhat depressed, complains about pounding headaches. After getting permission from therapist to use medication, he reports that after leaving the last session, he was depressed and sobbed for awhile. He explains it as a delayed reaction to the discussion about his brother, stressing his hurt about brother's rejection of him. Therapist interprets the hurt feelings as a reaction to guilt about jealousy and hostility to brother and that the headaches and depressed feelings are a method of punishing himself for hostility. Patient finally brings out that attacking his brother is like attacking himself. There is an intellectual discussion between therapist and patient about patient's identification with his brother and his ambivalence toward him.

Session No. 31 (22 May 1958)

Patient discusses his rivalrous feelings toward brother and his displacement of anger from brother to sister and to wife. He points out the disadvantage of being a younger brother and then veers to the advantages when therapist points out his ambivalence to brother. Both patient and therapist work on patient's ambivalent feelings toward brother and wife. Patient finally admits his admiration for wife. Therapist connects this ambivalence with patient's impotence. Patient, sighing sadly, accepts therapist's formulation and the session, which was predominantly warm and friendly, ends with therapist wishing patient a good weekend.

Session No. 32 (26 May 1958)

Patient discusses with satisfaction his justifiable anger toward mother. He claims that he was gratified with therapist's statement the last session that even though he was not the favorite of his parents, he was not necessarily inferior to his siblings. Apparently this increased his self-esteem to the extent that he can visualize confronting his mother with her hostile behavior toward him, chancing the possibility of a rift with her. Therapist points out that this is a struggle for emancipation on the part of patient. When therapist forcefully adds that patient wants wife to be dependent on his mother instead of on him, patient disagrees and protests, but finally agrees with therapist. There is an attempt on the part of therapist to temper this interpretation by laughter and warmth.

Session No. 33 (29 May 1958)

Therapist makes a conscious effort to increase patient's self-esteem by criticizing mother, whom he labels a "controlling man-eating shark" who contributed to patient's difficulties. After patient complains that wife neglects her appearance, therapist focuses on wife's dependent needs. He then emphasizes the positive elements in patient and urges him to be more mature, effective, and productive. Patient registers satisfaction at therapist's approval of him and agrees with everything that therapist says.

Session No. 34 (2 June 1958)

After patient talks about a person with a sibling problem similar to his, therapist discusses with him his negative reaction to brother, which he ties to patient's hostility, dependency, and guilt. Patient, tense and embarrassed, discloses his fantasy of his wish to lean on a strong virile man and labels it homosexual, although he denies erotic feelings. Both therapist and patient discuss the dynamics of such feelings as connected with passivity and dependence on brother, who was aggressive and independent. At therapist's request for further association, patient obligingly relates the wish to lean on strong men. Therapist, in a kindly reassuring manner, points out that patient still has problems and dependency needs and connects it with transference, but adds that it is a temporary state. He thus gives patient hope that he can develop adequate strength with the help of treatment.

Session No. 35 (5 June 1958)

In a mutually warm atmosphere, patient continues to focus on his rivalrous feelings toward brother. In his enthusiasm, he ignores therapist's comments and continues to describe his general improvement, stressing his increased self-esteem, increased sexual drive, and potency. When therapist finally gets in a statement that patient still has a good deal to work through, patient becomes submissive, but recaptures his previous aggressive trend by maintaining that he is less dependent than before.

Session No. 36 (9 June 1958)

Patient continues discussing the problem of being a younger brother. Therapist repeatedly stresses patient's rivalry with brother and his dependence, hostility, and guilt toward the latter. Therapist attempts to convey to patient through intellectual formulations the dynamic reasons for his symptoms, stressing patient's ambivalence to brother. Patient cooperates by entering into the search. He is reflective, ruminates, and at times looks puzzled as if he didn't quite grasp therapist's request. Toward the end of the session patient insistently inquires as to when therapist plans to interrupt treatment, thus disclosing his anxiety, which is somewhat allayed when therapist informs him that he will not leave for several weeks.

Session No. 37 (12 June 1958)

Therapist, twenty minutes late, apologizes. Patient, after some blocking, reluctantly and in an embarrassed manner brings out his recent interest in the physical strength of both men and women. He reviews the past, when after being successful as a man and in his work, he became depressed and discouraged in a former job. Therapist interprets this regression as being due to patient's inability to accept success and his need for punishment. Patient obligingly admits anxiety about present successes. There is an interchange between therapist and patient about the role brother played in the above. Therapist is active as he stresses his point, ignoring patient's attempt to contribute. When at last patient describes the difficulties he has had with a woman superior, therapist again confronts him with his dependent strivings and his self-punitive measures, which follow success. Patient in a half-hearted way, agrees with therapist, but states that he feels guilty for being dependent.

Session No. 38 (19 June 1958)

Patient continues his compliant and dependent deferential attitude toward the therapist, who behaves in a somewhat paternal, omniscient manner and makes many lengthy interpretations, some of which appear speculative. The chief theme is patient's awareness of his dependent relationship on his brother, of which he is ashamed. The transference situation is lightly touched upon when therapist points out that patient expects intellectual feeding from the therapist. Although therapist interprets patient's intellectualization as a defense, he, himself, indulges in intellectualization. When the therapist appears to minimize patient's success, patient gently reproaches therapist and succeeds in having therapist modify his position.

Session No. 39 (23 June 1958)

Patient, possibly to please therapist, begins by proudly reporting an incident in which he was quite assertive with his wife in expressing his wish that she spend the weekend with him instead of with her family. Therapist, however, continues to focus on the theme of dependency. When the therapist has difficulty understanding the details of what patient was trying to communicate, the patient continues to be compliant without expressing any irritation at therapist's difficulty in understanding him. Therapist seems to be overlooking other emotional conflicts in patient's material, and, toward the end of the session, appears to arrive at an impasse, which he attempts to solve by asking patient direct questions about his wife and about dreams. Patient does not express his feelings about being misunderstood and compliantly agrees and tries to remember his dreams for the therapist.

Session No. 40 (26 June 1958)

Patient reports tension and anxiety, which prove to be related to feelings of anger toward therapist, and fears of his own passive dependency, which patient relates to homosexual feelings. Therapist, however, avoids the subject of homosexuality. When patient compliantly returns to the theme of dependency and his fear of expressing anger lest he lose dependency, therapist takes patient's intellectual formulations for emotional insights and is obviously pleased. Patient's anxiety and tension appear to be considerably less at the end of the session than at the beginning.

Session No. 41 (30 June 1958)

Patient apparently complies with therapist's suggestion in session No. 39 by bringing in a dream. Again therapist makes many interpretations, few of which are based on any associations made by patient. Therapist does not comment on patient's feminine identification and the homosexual theme evident in the associations. Patient's attitude continues to be a wish to accept and confirm therapist's interpretations. Patient apparently wants to show therapist he is improving and more accepting of his wife, and on one occasion succeeds in getting therapist to give him recognition for more mature behavior toward his wife over the weekend. On several occasions patient did make feeble attempts to disagree with therapist; this related to his objecting to therapist's comment that he had dreamed similar content previously.

Session No. 42 (3 July 1958)

Patient reports a dream in which he castigates his father for being a bad father. Therapist interprets the dream as an expression of anger toward the therapist. This emboldens patient to express some criticism of therapist, referring to the previous session. Therapist accepts and encourages expression of negative feelings, indicating that patient may feel that therapist is failing him, just as his father had failed him. Patient, after expressing his longing for a good father, briefly expresses some anger at the therapist for "refusing to be a good father" and begins talking about his mother. When the patient relates the emotional deprivation he experienced in childhood in relation to his parents, therapist's behavior is noticeably warm and emphatic. Therapist makes many theoretical interpretations about patient's relations to mother and father and patient compliantly accepts therapist's interpretations.

Session No. 43 (7 July 1958)

At the beginning of the session patient states that he has been becoming more tense and relates this aggravation of anxiety to therapy. However, almost immediately he apologetically reassures the therapist that he knows this occurs to everyone in therapy. The main content of the session refers to patient's dream—about a wealthy, eccentric woman like the mad woman of Chaillot—and to patient's original fear of his aggressive mother. Therapist makes many interventions centering around patient's feelings about his mother and reassures patient that there really is no longer any need for him to fear his mother. When the therapist states that patient's angry feelings really belong in the past, patient compliantly agrees with therapist. Therapist makes no reference to patient's nonverbalized longing, anxiety, and negative feelings, which all observers believed were related to the impending two-month's vacation.

Session No. 44 (10 July 1958)

Patient complains of headaches, is anxious and blocked. He returns to the dream of the previous session, expressing surprise at how much he feared his mother's anger. Therapist points out that patient may expect therapist to be rejecting, just as his mother was. Patient then compares his feelings for his mother and for his father. When patient, after some hesitation, states that his feelings may relate to therapist, the therapist helps patient express such feelings by stating that his blocking may have to do with anger at therapist because he may feel that therapist does not give him sufficient support, especially since therapist is leaving on a two-month vacation. Patient states that he felt like sobbing in the previous session when he was talking about his resentment toward his father. When patient refers to the dream of the previous session, in which the mad woman was doing something to him, he states that he becomes upset. Therapist then goes on to give a long discussion centering around patients triangular relationship with mother and father. Patient appears upset. Therapist was warm, supportive, and friendly all through the session.

Session No. 45 (14 July 1958)

Patient complains of being tense and depressed. He interprets this as due to oedipal feelings that were stirred up in the last session. Therapist focuses on the underlying "passive-dependent feminine longings'' that patient presumbly experiences toward therapist. Repeated interpretation that patient focuses intellectually on the oedipal conflict in order to avoid the less acceptable fear of his role as a man, and therefore relates to his father, brother, and therapist in a passive-dependent manner, is strongly fended off by patient who feels that therapist is implying that he is basically a homosexual. His anxiety is not allayed despite the therapist's effort to reassure him on this score, especially after a later interpretation that patient's mother intuitively sensed the patient's feminine identification, and that this was why she had kicked him—because she resented his refusing to be the man she wanted. Patient appears to be in considerable anxiety at the end of the session.

Session No. 46 (17 July 1958)

After the previous session patient felt panicky and phoned the therapist for reassurance. Therapist reassured him over the phone that his panic was due to the impending interruption of the therapy.

The session opens with patient expressing some dissatisfaction with therapist, stating that therapist has failed to understand that patient, because of his fear of the aggressive and seductive mother, wants protection from father and men. Patient also protests the interpretation that he was seeking a passive-feminine relationship with his father and therapist and expresses fear about homosexuality. Therapist reassures him that he is not homosexual. Team infers though that he acts out his receptive longings when he asks for and receives an additional session.

Session No. 47 (21 July 1958)

Patient again reveals how anxiety-provoking the dependency interpretation has been for him because of its homosexual implications by stating that he had sexual relations with his wife to prove to himself that he can be a man without therapist's help. His discouragement and depression gives way to angry compliants about therapist's interpretation, which hurt his sense of masculinity. Therapist was quite reassuring, made several direct suggestions and spoke of the coming interruption of therapy as a virtue and a benefit to patient, coming at this particular time. It is not clear to some of the observers whether therapist actually believed this, or whether this is merely more support for patient. Once again when patient reveals fear connected with feminine-passive longings, therapist gives reassurance by playing down the sexual aspect of such longings. Patient continues to act out his dependency needs by asking advice up to the very last minute of the session.

Therapist-Patient Interaction

After the ten-day interruption, the interpersonal relationship continues essentially as before. Patient makes no reference to the interruption and attempts to manipulate therapist into the sympathetic (parental) role by means of an essentially complaining and demanding attitude. However, he meets with no success and thereafter cooperates in the intellectual work. Although therapist's manner is largely kindly and accepting, he steadily exerts pressure on patient to give up his "wanting" attitudes. At one point he implies that the patient is more worthy than his sister. Patient appears visibly gratified and the assumption seems warranted that patient feels more valued than his sister by therapist. In the following Session, No. 30, patient succeeds in getting therapist to give him advice about medication for headaches, and thereafter compliantly cooperates with therapist in discussions focused mainly on patient's relationship with his brother. As before, therapist ignores patient's sad hurt feelings connected with his frustrated wish for love from his brother but encourages him in a permissive way to express his hostile feelings toward his brother.

Patient's behavior is compliant and in Session No. 31, he reveals awareness of his ambivalence toward his brother. The emotional climate is one of warmth and rapport, as therapist, according to his work sheet, enjoys the session and is pleased with patient's performance in acquiring these insights. Therapist is also pleased with himself for his good-humored tolerant, "understanding of patient's political philosophy," which differs from his own. Patient is apparently feeling accepted by and approved of by therapist, and in Session No. 32, reports, in a somewhat childlike way, that his self-esteem has been "boosted" by therapist's implication that he is not inferior to his siblings. He experiences some wounding of his self-esteem as a result of therapist's persistent forceful confrontations about dependency, and therapist's implication about not wanting to be a man. Patient disagrees and protests but finally agrees, but at the same time seems to recognize therapist's desire for him to emancipate himself from his mother and apparently wants to achieve this.

In Sessions No. 33 and No. 34, therapist, perhaps reacting to his increased forcefulness during the previous hour, is conspicuously warm, emphatic, supportive, and encouraging; he actively attempts to enhance patient's masculine self-esteem and to improve patient's self-image by focusing on some of patient's accomplishments and improvements and by covertly conveying some respect and regard for patient as a man and a person. In his work sheet therapist states he does this deliberately to "give patient support in his struggle for emancipation." It is the team's impression that he also offers himself as a masculine model by using "man to man" talk and by giving descriptions and explanations about mature behavior. Patient's verbal and nonverbal expressions reveal pleasure and gratitude as he receives these signs of regard from this idealized parent figure. Therapist is very accepting when patient reveals some "feminine" and "homosexual" tendencies, and patient feels relieved and reassured when the criticism and disapproval he clearly expected does not materialize. At the same time therapist again conveys his hope that patient will master these tendencies, but indicates that he does not expect "one hundred percent functioning as yet."

The next session (No. 35) is somewhat unusual, as patient, excited by some discoveries connected with a woman he knows who is in therapy, takes the lead and is permitted by therapist to be the more active one. The customary relationship is reestablished, however, in Sessions No. 36 and No. 37, with therapist in the active, at times forceful, role presenting patient with explanations and formulations and patient receptively and submissively cooperating in the predominantly intellectual activity. Patient expresses an anxious wish to continue the sessions as long as possible before the summer vacation and receives reassurances from therapist.

In Session No. 38, patient's attitude continues to be predominantly a passive-submissive one, except at one point when therapist seems depreciatory. He then asserts himself and succeeds in getting therapist to give him credit for successfully making progress and in getting therapist to be more understanding and empathic about his dependency problems. Although therapist accepts this self-assertion and yields to patient, several days later, in Session No. 39, he implicitly minimizes some newly assertive behavior with his wife that patient proudly reports, by interpreting it as a protest against dependency. There is some disagreement among members of the team as to whether, in therapist's persistent emphasis on "dependency," he is ignoring affectional needs and feelings relayed in patient's communications about his outside relationships.

In Session No. 40, when patient is tense and anxious, and when the material clearly suggests that the anxiety is connected with "homosexuality," (patient's word) and his feminine identifications, therapist seems to avoid this subject. Patient follows suit, and in his customary compliant way participates in discussing aggression, guilt, fear, and dependency. Therapist, whose manner is on the whole friendly and reassuring, is pleased with what he considers to be the patient's insight. Patient's tensions subside as the session progresses, possibly because of therapist's reassuringly friendly behavior, or possibly because the "homosexuality" has been minimized by being ignored.

In the following session (No. 41), therapist again ignores patient's feminine identification, which is clearly revealed in a dream, and the "homosexuality," and focuses again on patient's wish to avoid the mature adult role. Therapist is active, warm, and friendly, and is clearly enjoying working with the dream, as revealed in his animated manner and by his statements in his work sheet. Patient is his usual receptive compliant self, accepting therapist's interpretations except for one interaction, consisting of patient successfully asserting himself and getting therapist to give him credit for some exceptionally mature and giving behavior with his wife over the weekend, which therapist had ignored. Having received credit from therapist for progress, patient's frustrated and unhappy feelings ostensibly subside and he appears satisfied. Patient's repressed resentment, however, appears in a dream in which he castigates his father for not having been a good father to him. Patient sadly expresses conscious desires for a good father such as, he assumes, therapist had; then briefly expresses some anger at therapist for refusing to be a good father to him. Presumably some of this anger is a reaction to the imminent summer vacation. Therapist is sympathetic, warm, and gentle and there is warm rapport between therapist and patient. Possibly therapist is reacting with empathic tenderness and gentleness to patient's unhappiness as he relates the emotional deprivation he experienced in childhood with both his parents.

In Session No. 43, some of patient's anger toward his original family members and his fear of his aggressive mother is expressed. Therapist's attitude is an encouraging, accepting one. In response to patient's somewhat naive question about whether or not he should act on his anger, therapist directs him not to, and implies that he should give these emotions up as they belong to the past.

In Session No. 45 therapist interprets that patient's passive-dependent longings in relation to therapist may have unconscious homosexual implications. Although references are made to patient's immediate feelings about therapist and the summer interruption in the therapy, therapist continues to focus primarily on patient's interaction with his parents and his passive-feminine strivings and his fear in relation to father and therapist. In his work sheet therapist gives the explanation that this is necessary because he considers patient's anxiety to be due to "this material being just below the surface." To the observing team therapist appears to be ignoring patient's intense anxiety in reaction to this interpretation and to patient's feelings about the impending interruptions. Following Session No. 45, patient develops panicky feelings, telephones therapist, and receives reassurance.

In the next session, No. 46, two days later, patient, angry and tense, verbalizes resentment toward therapist, claiming therapist has let him down, and defends against therapist's interpretations about homosexuality by protesting and stressing his incestuous sexual feelings toward his mother and his liking for some women colleagues. Therapist firmly but warmly persists in his interpretations, but now emphasizes the interruption in the therapy as contributing to patient's passive-feminine wishes for a father. Patient ignores all this and persistently presses for reassurance that he is not a homosexual, and also for an additional hour before the interruption, both of which are finally given to him by therapist. It is possible that this successful self-assertion is also reassuring to patient.

In the final session (No. 47) before the summer interruption, therapist, after some initial annoyance, is a warm, giving, father substitute who gratifies patient's demands for reassurance about his progress in therapy and about his masculinity, but at the same time communicates by actions and words that he considers it necessary for patient to face and give up his dependent feminine tendencies. He attempts in a helpful way to diminish the narcissistic blow and the anxiety by appropriate explanations. Patient appears relieved, but the nonverbal cues indicate that sadness, as well as anxiety and anger, are present.

It is to be noted that patient is not expressing his feelings about the interruption itself, as he has to deal primarily with therapist's interpretations about his feminine identifications and wishes. It appears to the team that therapist is, to a considerable extent, avoiding patient's feelings about therapist in the transference. As on previous occasions, therapist suggests that the interruption will be helpful and that he will take the interruption well.

At the end of the session patient appears relieved but his actions reveal a reluctance to leave and he arranges to get a final bit of receptive gratification by asking therapist if he should analyze on his own.

Therapeutic Experience of the Patient

In the Interpersonal Relationship with Therapist

Patient's therapeutic experience in the interpersonal relationship remains essentially the same as in Sessions No. 22–28. Therapist continues on the whole to be a kindly, reassuring, accepting parent-surrogate who wants patient to mature and who offers himself as a mature, masculine model; who implicitly disapproves patient's remaining infantile dependent strivings and "complaining and demanding attitudes," and exerts steady pressure on him to give them up. In the twenty-ninth hour patient receives the implication from therapist that patient may be more worthy than either his sister or his brother, even though the parents may have shown preference for the other siblings. Patient reacts with "boosting" of his self-esteem, so that we may assume that this is a corrective emotional experience for patient in contrast to the experience that he has had with his own parents. When, in response to therapist's implicit and explicit expectations, patient manages to behave more maturely but then fails to get overt credit from therapist, patient successfully insists on a number of occasions in forcing recognition from therapist for his accomplishments. Patient experiences the usual gratification throughout this period of joining in the intellectual work of the therapy with therapist's approval. Although passively submissive for the most part, he shows a gradually increasing ability to assert himself toward therapist without retaliation from therapist. He is also able to express resentment toward members of his family, with therapist's acceptance, although therapist states that those feelings "belong to the past" and implies that they should be given up. At the same time patient continues to experience the fact that acceptance of therapist's intellectual formulations is usually followed by approval and pleasure on therapist's part.

Another significant therapeutic experience occurs in Session No. 34, when therapist noncritically accepts patient's embarrassed exposure of "feminine homosexual" fantasies. An equally significant experience in the same session is therapist's moderation of his customary pressure upon patient when he recognizes that patient's changing is not expected to be either immediate or "100 percent." As the summer separation period approaches, patient experiences therapist's attitude that such vacations are good for him and that he should accept them without strong feelings about the interruption or about therapist. This may also be regarded as a significant element in the model of maturity that is being presented to patient by therapist. As usual, patient, after a struggle, ostensibly complies with therapist's wishes.

Thus, in the interpersonal relationship, therapist essentially is a parent figure whose personal affairs make it necessary for him to leave his child for several months, and who helps his child master (and repress) his anxiety, frustration, anger, and sadness by means of reassurances, encouragement, and the expression of confidence in the child's ability to get along without him. Patient, in turn, like the child who responds positively and compliantly, masters (suppresses and represses) his anxieties and other emotions, feels relieved, and, realizing that he has no alternative in the face of the parent's firmness, complies with the parent's wishes, reconciles himself (at least consciously) to the inevitable and makes the best of it.

New or Increased Awarenesses

During this period patient acquired an increased intellectual awareness of the following:

1. Better understanding of his past and present relationships with his mother, sister, and brother, with special emphasis on his mother's favoring his sister over both him and his brother.
2. Better understanding of his tendency to repress his competitive, resentful feelings toward his brother and other men, with resultant self-depreciation, depression, and regression to passive dependency; also a better understanding of his ambivalent feelings toward his brother, his tendency to idealize his brother, and his difficulty, as a younger brother, to achieve a sense of his own separate identity.
3. His ambivalent wishes toward his wife, particularly as regards dominance and submissiveness in relationship to her.
4. His mother's ambivalence to him, but particularly her hostile and rejecting attitudes, and his turning to and being disappointed by his father, with consequent increased yearnings for paternal love; also the relationship of the onset of his stuttering to an incident in which he was beaten and kicked by his mother at age thirteen.
5. Hostility and guilt as underlying factors in his headaches and depressions; increased insight into his conflict between expressing and not expressing anger, namely, that if he asserts himself he loses his dependent gratification, yet if he fails to do so he loses his self-esteem. Intellectual

acceptance of therapist's formulation concerning conflict over success in terms of (a) guilt and (b) his wish not to give up dependent gratifications.

6. His inhibitions and compulsive tendencies and their relationship to his experiences with his controlling mother.

7. His inhibition of spontaneity, warmth, and passion in the sexual relationship with his wife.

8. His longings for a good father in the transference and his dependent yearnings in relationship to the therapist-father; therapist's expectations that he relinquish these; and a beginning awareness of his anxiety that his passive-dependent longings in relationship to therapist may have some unconscious homosexual implications.

Symptomatic or Behavioral Changes

1. Continuing sexual potency
2. Gradually increasing assertiveness and emancipation from brother and mother
3. Increasing self-esteem and lessening self-depreciation
4. Increasing sense of his own identity as separate from his older brother
5. Increasing ability to assert himself in relationship to therapist
6. A more giving and assertive relationship to his wife and children

These changes appear to be the result of a combination of factors involving insights and working through, and the effects of the interpersonal experience with the therapist as follows:

As the patient has become increasingly aware of his immature patterns and strivings, and of some of their consequences, shame and to some extent guilt motivate him toward more rational and mature attitudes and behavior. Diminution of guilt occurs as he develops more realistic evaluations of his past and present interpersonal relationships, especially with his parents and siblings and of the justification of some of his resentments and self-assertion. Increased aggression can occur as his improved reality-testing in real experiences with the therapist and other individuals demonstrates that his now conscious fears of punishment (especially rejection) are unfounded. Patient's compliant tendencies, his wish, predominantly unconscious, to gain and to maintain the therapist-parent figure's acceptance, approval, and probably love, motivate him to conform to therapist's explicit wishes and demands to give up his immature patterns and to develop more adult masculine attitudes. Some identification with therapist and incorporation of his standards and wishes concerning the adult masculine role, thus reinforcing patient's already existing mature standards and values, are probably occurring.

Comparison between Observers and Therapist

In this block of sessions, the conspicuous difference between the team's and the therapist's evaluations lies in the therapist's almost exclusive emphasis on the patient's intrapersonal (intrapsychic) processes, including his insights, in contrast to the team's emphasis on what it considers to be the significant interpersonal transactions in addition to the patient's intrapersonal processes. The therapist, in contrast to the team, describes very few of the patient's actions and emotions as reactions to specific actions and attitudes of the therapist, but rather as reactions to some intrapsychic psychodynamic process connected with internal conflict and past experiences and relationships. As an example, in describing Session No. 29, after a ten-day interruption, the therapist states that the central issue is the patient's effort to please the analyst by verbally agreeing with him, and that when he "feels that the analyst sees through this," he tries to intellectualize as a defense, and that what is repressed is hostile jealousy toward the brother. The therapist states, "the formula is, as soon as he abandons the dependent, inferior role, he runs into competition with the brother."

The team's analysis of the session is as follows: The therapist and the patient seem to be in a struggle wherein the patient, although admitting improvement, complains bitterly about symptoms and the therapist confronts the patient with his complaining and demanding attitudes. The therapist urges the patient to give up his dependent demands, and the patient manipulates the situation in the hope of receiving from the therapist what he wanted as a child from his parents, a sympathetic parental attitude. However, he meets with no success and thereafter cooperates with the therapist in the cognitive-intellectual work, including discussions about competitive feelings toward brother and sister. From these observations the team regards the patient's intellectual activities as primarily motivated at this point by his unconscious wish to comply with the therapist's obvious desire for this kind of activity, while the therapist considers it as a defense against hostile jealousy feelings.

Another example in the same session is the team's describing that at one point the therapist implies that the patient may be more worthy than either his brother or his sister, even though the parents may have shown a preference for them. The patient reacted with visible gratification, from which the team makes the assumption that he felt valued by the therapist and experienced a "boosting" of his self-esteem. Many similar examples of interpersonal interactions are described by the team, but not by the therapist.

The major specific difference in the description of the therapeutic experience is as follows: The team specifically describes the interpersonal relationship as one in which the therapist continues on the whole to be a kindly, reassuring, accepting parent-surrogate, who clearly wants the patient to mature and who offers himself as a mature masculine model; who implicitly disapproves of the patient's remaining infantile dependent strivings and complaining and demanding attitudes, and exerts steady pressure on him to give them up. In response to the therapist's implicit and explicit expectations, the patient manages to behave more maturely—and then on a number of occasions even insisted assertively on getting credit or recognition from the therapist when it was not forthcoming. The team describes the gratification that the patient gets in the largely intellectual work with the therapist. It also describes the patient's increasing self-assertion toward the therapist without encountering any hostile response. Neither of these are mentioned in the therapist's evaluation. Most of the time the therapist describes the content of his verbal interventions, that is, the explicit overt interpretative element, and not the implicit, subtle nonverbal elements in the communications. There are some exceptions, such as his describing that he gave reassurances to the patient about homosexuality in the forty-sixth session. The final (forty-seventh) session of this block of sessions is an illustration. This was the final session before the summer interruption of the therapy (by the therapist). In his description, the therapist states that he explained to the patient that his dependent needs toward a father image originated in the past, that he is stronger now than he wants to admit, and that he will do well during the interruption. In contrast, the team's description is as follows:

> It is to be noted that the patient is not given much opportunity to express his feelings about the interruption itself, as he has to deal primarily with the therapist's interpretations about his feminine identifications and wishes. It appears that the therapist is, to a considerable extent, avoiding the patient's feelings (the presence of which can be inferred by a number of observable nonverbal cues) about the therapist in the transference. As on previous occasions, the therapist suggests that the interruption will be helpful and that the patient will take it well.
>
> At the end of the session, the patient appears relieved, but his actions reveal a reluctance to leave, and he arranges for a final bit of receptive gratification by asking the therapist if he should analyze on his own.

The team infers from its observations that the patient experiences the therapist's attitude that such vacations are good for him and that he should accept them without strong personal feelings about the interruption and the therapist. This should be regarded as a significant element in the model of maturity that is being presented to the patient by the therapist. The team also notes that "as usual, the patient, after a struggle, ostensibly complies with the therapist's wishes." The team's analysis of this episode is as follows:

> Thus, in the interpersonal relationship the therapist essentially is a parent figure whose personal affairs make it necessary for him to leave his child for several months, and who helps his child master (and suppress) his anxiety, frustration, anger, and sadness by means of reassurances, encouragement, and the expression of confidence in the child's ability to get along without him. The patient, in turn, is like the child who responds positively and compliantly, masters (suppresses) his anxieties and other emotions, feels relieved, and, realizing that he has no alternative in the face of the parent's firmness, complies with the parent's wishes, reconciles himself (consciously) to the inevitable and makes the best of it.

Although the therapist focuses only rarely on the immediate interpersonal interaction as it occurs during the sessions, in his evaluation he describes his general conscious emotional attitude toward the patient as follows: "The therapist's initial lack of sympathy with this type of personality (highly dependent, intellectualizing) has greatly diminished. The therapist subjectively can account for this mainly by his growing intellectual curiosity in the patient's dynamics, the gratification he receives from the patient being a rather understanding and quite intelligent person. The patient also must have pleased the analyst by the fact that he made such good progress. The therapist also begins to recognize certain latent strengths in the patient, which he did not expect, and also finds his intellectual honesty appealing. In spite of this, there seems to be a residue of lack of emotional enthusiasm which self-inspection shows appears to be a residue of negative feelings toward this type of personality who intellectualizes everything and cannot commit himself to any action or any human relationship with a wholesome decision." This introspective account of the therapist's conscious attitude toward the patient is consistent with the team's description of the therapist's behavior as "on the whole, a kindly reassuring accepting parent-surrogate."

In comparing the team's and the therapist's description of the insights acquired during this block of hours, there is considerable agreement about the content, (see Sessions No. 29–47, Therapeutic Experience of the Patient). The therapist describes the internal psychodynamic cycle of dependence-shame-competitive aggression-guilt, and states that the patient "recognized it both intellectually and experientially by repeating it in the treatment toward the therapist." The team regards the "new and increased awareness" as largely cognitive-intellectual, and in some instances as compliant acceptance on the intellectual level of the therapist's formulations.

10

Therapy—Sessions 48–64

Summary of Manifest Events

Session No. 48 (29 September 1958)

In this first session after the summer interruption, patient speaks of having done beautifully, and then proceeds with examples that tend to deny this. There was considerable intellectual discussion about the conflict between his "idealistic" values and his original family's "materialistic" values, and his recognition of the relationship of rage and guilt toward his brother. When therapist related patient's rage to his unresolved dependency-independence conflict vis-à-vis his original family circle, patient readily agreed. Therapist terminated the session abruptly and somewhat early.

Session No. 49 (2 October 1958)

Therapist tries to get patient to admit his anger at having the previous session cut short, and to discuss how in the transference situation he repeats the wish to please, be accepted by, and be dependent on therapist. Therapist is kind and gentle to patient. Toward end of session, therapist continues the interpretation of previous session regarding patient's conflict of dependency on mother, versus independent strivings, with loyalty to his wife. Therapist indicates that patient's leaning over backward to avoid asking any favors of mother is not genuine independence, but a wish to prove his independence and proof that dependency on mother is still something he feels he has to guard against.

Session No. 50 (6 October 1958)

Indicating that he is speaking as one adult to another, therapist repeats the interpretation of the past two sessions—that marriage is a chronic emotional strain on patient, producing anger because part of patient wishes to maintain his infantile dependency. Therapist suggests to patient that he accept the fact that he is dependent, and not to expect therapist to completely dissolve such longings in therapy. It seems that patient feels hurt and criticized by therapist for being dependent and appears startled, but makes only a feeble protest. Therapist appears annoyed by patient's dependency demands and gives the impression that he feels they cannot be entirely overcome in therapy. Therapist again terminates session prematurely.

Session No. 51 (9 October 1958)

Patient angrily reproaches therapist for being critical of him in the previous session. He feels therapist considers him a weakling who cannot recover in therapy. Patient feels that therapist underestimates his strengths. Patient also emphasizes that therapy has made him worse in some respects, since he now has more body tensions and depressions than he had prior to therapy. Therapist returns to the transference interpretation of the forty-ninth session by pointing out that patient wishes to ingratiate himself with therapist, and only afterwards will he admit to difficulties during the summer interruption in therapy. Therapist repeats interpretation of previous session about the need to accept oneself with human weakness, and that it is a sign of strength to do so. Patient feels therapist considers him helpless, weak, and dependent and was able to accuse therapist of calling him weak when he calls him dependent overtly, even though therapist made this interpretation in a kindlier way than in the previous session and gives patient support regarding his strengths.

Session No. 52 (13 October 1958)

Patient complains of anxiety at the idea of his dependency, and fears that he may give in to such longings. Both therapist and patient engage in intellecutal discussion as to the origin of patient's distaste for dependency. Therapist explains the disadvantage of overcompensating for dependency needs or denying them, instead of learning to live with them. Therapist asserts that patient could now accept his brother on equal terms and that "mother is no longer important." Patient introduces the homosexual theme, admitting he fears affectionate and warm feelings to therapist and brother as a sign of weakness and homosexuality. Patient then relates a dream about beating up his sister and brother-in-law in the presence of his mother, and felt good about it because he felt this proved he could assert himself. Therapist is warm and firm and gives many suggestions and explanations and permissive reassurances regarding affection feelings to brother.

Session No. 53 (16 October 1958)

Patient complains of tension and headaches, which he attributes to failure to gain recognition. He expresses his confusion about therapist's contradictory attitudes to his dependency needs. Therapist differentiates patient's need to get recognition from feelings of dependency. Therapist interprets that patient is angry with therapist for exposing his overcompensatory denial of his underlying dependency needs. Therapist interprets patient's dream of the previous session as a wish to prove his strength to save his pride. Patient explains that the reason he is basically a hostile person is because his mother did not permit him to express anger. Therapist returns to the discussion of dependency and the related need for recognition and approval and reassures patient as to his competence, indicating he should not need the recognition he seeks. Therapist returns to the dream of the previous session, with both therapist and patient theorizing on its various interpretations. Therapist is fatherly and tolerant and patient appears happy with therapist. Therapist cut this session short after thirty-eight minutes, stating that it was necessary for him to catch a train and patient smilingly accepts this.

Session No. 54 (20 October 1958)

Therapist shows much interest in patient's minor car accident. Patient describes premature ejaculation and lack of sexual interest with consequent depression and loss of self-esteem, and increase in his needs for dependency. Therapist insists that patient's dependency needs are not really stronger now, but awareness of them make them seem stronger. Patient again reproaches therapist indirectly by stating that therapy makes him worse, more depressed and less patient, because defenses against dependency are stripped. Therapist agrees with patient that patient uses sex to compensate for loss of self-esteem and reassures patient that he is successful, does not have to prove anything, and that to have dependency needs does not make a weak person in all areas. Therapist relates patient's anxiety about dependency to patient's relation with his brother. Patient receives considerable gratification from therapist's reassurance, supportiveness and "giving." (Session lasts 51 minutes.)

Session No. 55 (23 October 1958)

Patient relates his anger at wife's giving to others instead of to him, and tells of dream in which he leaves his wife. Patient apparently tries to please therapist by trying to give therapist "the correct answers." Therapist asked patient to "feel, not to think." There is discussion relating to this dream, leading to the interpretation that patient obtains unconscious gratification from his submissive dependent attitudes toward brother and therapist, as well as toward wife and mother. Patient regards therapist's comments as depreciation similar to those of brother and mother. Therapist responds by reassuringly stressing patient's adequacy, and states one can have dependent wishes at times and still not be "a nincompoop." Therapist adds, "We all hate responsibilities at times." Patient is pleased by this comment. Therapist is warm and soothing. Patient basks in therapist's acceptance.

Session No. 56 (27 October 1958)

Patient seems ashamed to admit that his anger is a result of the demands the family makes on him. Patient recognizes more clearly his identification with his sons and his brother, and realizes his death wishes toward his younger son relate to similar wishes toward brother.

Therapist states patient wants everyone to make up to him for what he missed as a child, but softens this by pointing out patient had justification for such feelings as a child. Therapist continues to be warm and supporting.

Session No. 57 (30 October 1958)

When patient tries but cannot recall content of the previous session, therapist reminds him. Patient then tells of his anger and sudden loss of sexual feeling toward his wife when she asked him to check on the children before lovemaking. He had premature ejaculation and felt headachy and insecure. Therapist interprets poor potency as due to angry feelings. Patient says he knows he competes with the children for his wife's favors. Therapist points out that patient wishes to perpetuate his dependency on therapist by appearing weak as he did with his brother. Therapist also raises the question of patient's hostile feelings toward therapist. Patient replies that any hostile feelings toward therapist are really directed toward his brother. Therapist interprets that patient's needs for dependency inhibit the angry feelings. Therapist continues to be friendly, discussing patient's anger toward therapist. In the course of this session, therapist casually asks patient how he would like to view a film calculated to bring out angry feelings.

Session No. 58 (3 November 1958)

Patient refers back to therapist's invitation to view a film about anger and feels that perhaps it is now unnecessary, since he has been feeling angry at his wife, tense and depressed with a superior. Therapist points out that patient doesn't permit himself to feel anger, but merely talks about it and patient recognizes that he submits to therapist to avoid irritating him, as he did with his brother. Patient's feeling that therapist might "throw him out of therapy" if he makes no progress is interpreted by therapist as an expression of a wish to be thrown out so that he can cling to his dependency, rather than resolve it. Therapist explains that patient repeats with therapist his relationship with his brother, using therapist as the critical, strong brother upon whom he can lean.

Session No. 59 (6 November 1958)

Patient reports having viewed the film and expresses genuine anger at therapist for not preparing him for being strapped to a table, hooked up, and treated as an experimental specimen. Patient states that he found it to be a humiliating, ghastly experience to watch the film in that helpless, passive position and that he felt asssaulted. Patient accuses therapist of being insensitive like his father and not really understanding or being involved or concerned with patient's feelings. Therapist explains the importance of the emotional experience of expressing anger without suffering any punishment. He then indicates that he considers patient's anger exaggerated. Patient's anger is diluted as therapist continues to discuss and interpret his anger. Although therapist acts as the tolerant father who accepts patient's expressions of rage, one of the observers thinks that the diminution of patient's anger was more the consequence of his own fear of cutting himself off from therapist's support and acceptance than it was of any significant discouragement from therapist.

Session No. 60 (10 November 1958)

Patient is able to express his critical feelings about therapist while justifying them as due to his need to be in the limelight, to be treated as the favored son. Therapist explains patient's need for recognition, going on to a transference interpretation by saying that patient wishes to defy therapist by minimizing his involvement in the film. Patient confirms this. Patient returns to a childish, compliant, begging attitude as he expresses the hope that the film was selected especially for him; therapist partially complies with this appeal. Therapist advises patient to express angry feelings in the therapeutic situation. Patient theorizes about competition with therapist as repetition of competition with his brother. Therapist is friendly and accepting of the competitive and hostile feelings toward therapist, not only by verbally encouraging such negative feelings but by indicating to patient that although he recognizes patient has such feelings, this in no way affects his attitude toward patient.

Session No. 61 (13 November 1958)

Patient complains of "feeling lousy" and headachy, and he thinks it is due to anger. As the discussion continues, patient becomes emotionally more upset and on the verge of tears. Patient feels embarrassed about it and struggles to control the tears. In spite of therapist's encouragement "to let himself go," patient controls his crying. Following this, therapist and patient talk about anger versus dependency and therapist consistently encourages patient to express anger.

Session No. 62 (17 November 1958)

Patient returns to the theme of his feelings toward therapist, especially the loss of self-esteem when therapist interprets his dependency. He feels that he must appear mature in order to win therapist's praise and that he "cannot win" with therapist. Therapist supports patient and interprets patient's intolerance of weakness in himself as being related to the unsuccessful rivalry with his brother that caused his mother to consider him "a nothing" and thus "annihilate him." The word *annihilate* disturbed patient, who admitted the word made him aware of the wish to annihilate therapist. When patient wonders why his angry feelings to therapist prior to the interview disappear on his seeing therapist, therapist interprets this as patient's fear of losing therapist if he expresses such angry feelings. This is similar to feelings he used to have toward his brother. Therapist announces there will be only two more sessions before Thanksgiving recess. Patient ends session by stating the anxiety he felt at the beginning of the session is relieved.

Session No. 63 (20 November 1958)

Patient states he felt very good until just before coming in for his session, when his tension and depression returned. Patient returns to his "annihilation" wishes toward therapist. Therapist relates patient's difficulty in expressing hostile feelings to therapist as being similar to the way he felt toward his brother, relating this to his fear of the consequences. Therapist points out patient's fear of separation from his brother and from therapist. Patient weeps after this talk of separation. Therapist continues to be friendly, kindly, and reassuring.

Session No. 64 (24 November 1958)

Patient reports somatic symptoms and relates them to therapist's impending vacation. He also discusses how he has become aware of the similarity of his feelings toward his brother and toward therapist. Therapist points out patient's struggle for the necessary emancipation versus his wish to nurture his dependency on wife, on brother, and on therapist by continuing to feel weak and have neurotic symptoms. Patient expresses "feeling heavy inside, like mourning" and weeps. Therapist is supportive and then patient states he feels better. Therapist explains that patient is mourning because he is losing his "internalized object, his strong brother which lives side by side with weak image of himself." Therapist adds that when patient will feel the equal of therapist or brother, he will no longer need this "foreign body, the internalized brother." Therapist closes session by saying he will see patient in two weeks. Patient thanks him and appears reassured.

Therapist-Patient Interaction

Therapy resumed after the long summer vacation. Patient's reactions to the interruption of the therapy, and to the resumption of therapy, are mentioned by patient but are not focused on by therapist. Therapist's activity is mainly directed toward trying to get patient to face what he considers to be patient's important conflicting dependency-independency feelings toward his original family. Patient prefers to focus on his increased independence and assertiveness during the summer, so that a struggle develops between patient and therapist. Patient's ingratiating behavior and covert wish to be accepted by therapist-parent is not commented on during the session, but is interpreted by therapist in the following Session, No. 49. When patient finally agrees with therapist about his seeking acceptance and support and admits his dependency wishes, therapist gives him credit for "doing much better" during the summer. Therapist is unusually kindly and gentle during this session as he makes his various interpretations. Patient is still afraid to express open criticism against therapist, although encouraged by therapist on several appropriate occasions to do so.

In Session No. 50, focusing again on dependent needs, therapist, with a kindly manner, for motives not apparent to the observers, advises patient not to expect to completely resolve his dependent longings during the therapy. Patient's expression shows surprise, hurt, and disappointment, and he states that he feels discouraged. From his statements in his work sheet, therapist is apparently having doubts about the patient changing his dependent tendencies and consciously uses this technique to diminish patient's "hopes and goals." Patient's further reactions appear in Session No. 51, when he directly and angrily accuses therapist of having been critical in the same way as his mother and brother, and of overlooking the mature part of him. Patient, clearly feeling depreciated by therapist, persistently asks whether therapist considers patient a weak person, and succeeds in getting reassurances from therapist about some of his assets and strengths. As on previous occasions, therapist tends to be accepting in the face of patient's anger. Therapist in his work sheet states he modified his interpretations about dependency to make them more acceptable.

In Session No. 52, patient is tense, anxious, and whining. There is much intellectual interchange centering around dependency, and the "homosexual meaning" of feeling affectionate toward his brother and toward therapist. Patient apparently derives considerable reassurance and relief of anxiety from therapist's many explanations, which indicate therapist's acceptance of some "dependency" on him, from therapist's giving patient permission to feel more affectionate toward his brother, and from therapist's essentially friendly, noncritical manner. Another possible factor is that the expected and feared punishment for his aggressiveness in Session No. 51 did not materialize.

In Session No. 53, patient verbalizes his need for recognition in his outside relationships. There is much intellectual discussion, with therapist giving many interpretations and explanations about patient's dependency conflicts. The parent-child transference relationship is lived out, with patient receiving gratification from the active, seemingly omniscient therapist-parent, who also gives patient recognition by reminding him that he is a good teacher. Patient continues essentially to live out the compliant submissive child role. At times he inhibits negative and aggressive reactions to the therapist-parent, including his reactions to therapist terminating sessions early on several occasions.

In Session No. 54, when patient, somewhat depressed, anxious, and despairing, reports lowered self-esteem and inferiority feelings connected with having had a premature ejaculation the previous night and with the discussions in the therapy about his "dependency," therapist provides much explicit reassurance about his adequacy as a person and a man. Therapist is very "giving" (even gives extra time, possibly an unconscious making amends for cutting previous session short). By the end of the session patient's mood improves; he explicitly states he feels reassured by therapist's acceptance of his "relapse," thus indicating that he preconsciously expected punishment (disapproval, rejection). Thus the parent-child transference relationship continues to be lived out. The observers have the impression that patient was avoiding the homosexual transference feelings.

In Session No. 55, therapist focuses on the patient's enjoyment of the submissive dependent role in his relationship with his brother and with therapist. When patient reacts by feeling depreciated, and explicitly compares therapist's behavior to his mothers' and brother's depreciation of him, therapist stresses patient's successes as a husband, father, and worker. Consistent with the child-parent transference and his immaturity, patient is manifestly relieved and gratified when therapist, who has been warm and kindly during the session, expresses acceptance and approval. In order to diminish patient's shame about his wish to be free of family responsibility, therapist implies that he and all men have similar wishes by stating that "we all want to be irresponsible at times and there is a child in all of us," thus implicitly approving and presenting a model for patient. Several members of the team have the impression that patient is successfully manipulating therapist into the role of reassuring supportive parent.

In Session No. 56, patient is receptive-dependent in a somewhat childlike way, and therapist seems to deliberately curb some mild irritability and behave in a patient, friendly, supportive manner while he carries on the work of helping patient achieve understandings. In Session No. 57, therapist and patient work well together discussing especially patient's problem of inhibiting anger, its relationship to his dependency needs, his idealization of his brother and of therapist, with whom he wants the subordinate dependent role, etc. Therapist is friendly, supportive, and, as usual, actively working at the task of helping patient achieve insights. Presumably in order to diminish the narcissistic conflict at the continued exposure of dependent strivings, therapist again calls patient's attention to the ubiquity of such strivings, even in Freud. He casually invites patient to witness a film* that will mobilize anger, and patient readily complies. Therapist's behavior implies more acceptance of patient as an equal, but at the same time therapist's unspoken wish for patient to give up his dependent strivings is communicated to patient repeatedly. He explicitly encourages patient to feel and express anger toward him, thus conveying his permissiveness.

In Session No. 58, therapist and patient mutually investigate patient's relationship with his brother and with therapist as an idealized brother figure, his dependent wishes, his wounded pride, his angry feelings, and his fear and inhibition of them, with patient playing a more active and less submissive role than usual. Patient's positive feelings and fear of rejection toward therapist are somewhat verbalized, but still largely lived out in the therapeutic situation. Therapist gives explicit reassurances that patient will not be rejected, and proceeds to explore and interpret the deeper motivations of this irrational fear. Patient continues to suppress most of his immediate negative emotional reactions in the interaction with

*This film was being shown as part of another research project.

therapist, but appears to have a greater conscious intellectual acceptance of, and theoretical understanding of, anger at therapist. Patient seems to feel relieved by therapist's permissive attitude about hostility and indicates a willingness, at least consciously, to come to grips with negative feelings toward therapist.

In Session No. 59, patient is furious and expresses strong resentment toward therapist for not preparing him for the unpleasant experience he underwent in the experiment with the film. He makes critical comments about therapist, accusing him of being insensitive and uninvolved like his father. Therapist, who is reassuring and warm throughout the session, is calmly accepting of patient's criticisms, but makes various interpretations about patient's anger, thus implying that it is not really justified. In addition, he explicitly contrasts his accepting attitude with patient's mother's and brother's critical one, and refers to this as a new experience for patient.

In Session No. 60, again referring to the film episode, patient complains that therapist treated him in an impersonal way; he then speaks of his need for recognition and love from his mother and his rivalry with brother for mother's approval and love. The main feature in the interpersonal relationship is patient's largely unverbalized, thwarted longing for loving treatment from therapist, his reactive anger, and his generally successful manipulation of therapist into giving him reassurances and gratifications that assuage his hurt pride and relieve his feelings of rejection. Overtly, patient and therapist engage in discussions that focus principally around needs for recognition, self-assertion, competition, and aggression. In these discussions therapist is friendly, reassuring, encouraging, and permissive about aggression. In patient's transference fantasies, therapist is apparently the "good" parental and fraternal figure whom patient is attempting with some success to manipulate into giving him signs of love and care, and from whom he fears rejection if he is openly demanding and aggressive.

Session No. 61 is a very emotional one. Patient is tense and depressed, and when speaking about competitive feelings and his dependent needs for therapist, has tears in his eyes. However, he inhibits his tears and his emotions, despite therapist's reassuring encouragement to freely express his feelings. During the rest of the session therapist, in a very warm, reassuring, encouraging, directing manner, attempts to get patient to express anger toward him, while patient appears like a frightened child who wants to comply with the strong parent's request but does not dare to do so. However, he does express his dissatisfaction and resentment about his own submissive compliant traits. He then receives reassuring suggestions from therapist that he should please himself in the therapy and that he will not be judged. In Session No. 62, the interpersonal interaction is essentially the same as in the previous session, with therapist repeatedly encouraging patient to express his "dependent" and angry feelings, and reassuring him that he will not be punished or rejected. Patient responds by expressing some thoughts about "annihilation" of therapist. During this session therapist informs patient that there will be two more sessions before a two-week Thanksgiving interruption.

In Session No. 63 patient expresses but does not elaborate upon his gratification that therapist accepts his hostile expressions, and states that it reminds him of past feelings when he was close to his brother. The inference can be made that patient-son is feeling more accepted by and probably loved by therapist-parent-brother. Again therapist communicates his wish for patient to express anger, and patient indicates his fears connected with anger. Following this, patient's warm feelings toward his brother and wish not to lose him are expressed, and it is apparent that patient has similar feelings toward therapist. Therapist reveals his covert desire for patient to "emancipate" himself. When therapist speaks of patient becoming mature and separating from therapist, patient cries, contemplating separation, and verbalizes sad feelings.

In Session No. 64, the final session before the two-week interruption, the important interpersonal interaction is patient's intense sadness and weeping in connection with the discussions about "emancipating" himself from his brother and the therapist, and presumably in connection with the upcoming two-week separation. Therapist is sympathetically accepting of patient's feelings and "mourning"; he gives various explanations and interpretations, and continues to firmly emphasize that patient should give up the "dependent" needs and relationships. Patient complies, intellectually accepting therapist's formulations about his grief being connected with separation from an "internalized brother image."

Therapeutic Experience of the Patient

In the Interpersonal Relationship

Patient's report, after the long summer vacation, of increased independence and assertiveness toward his original family, is met by a somewhat forceful focusing by therapist on patient's continued dependency attitudes. Patient at first struggles against this but then accepts it. In the next session, therapist softens this narcissistic blow and becomes very kind, gentle, and giving to patient. In Session No. 50 patient is surprised by an entirely new approach from therapist, who tells him he must not expect to completely resolve his dependent longings and should learn to accept himself more as he is. Patient experiences this as a depreciation of himself and reacts with feelings of rejection and discouragement, followed in the next session by angry associations that therapist is critical like mother and brother, and that therapist is overlooking the mature part of him. Therapist's response to patient's repeated demands for reassurance is a reparative one—he is warm and supportive, permissively reassures patient that "we all have weaknesses" thus offering himself as an object to identify with.

During the next seven sessions (52–58) patient's therapeutic experience with therapist is essentially an elaboration of the above. Therapist continues to be a warm, supportive, and encouraging but firm parent-surrogate who endeavors to differentiate between regressive, infantile dependency, which is not acceptable, and realistic dependency, which is. In response to Patient's report of lowered self-esteem, therapist gives explicit recognition to patient's abilities and adequacy, and treats patient as an equal on several occasions by discussing professional subjects with him. He permits and encourages patient to express open resentment and criticism of him without fear of retaliation, despite which patient tends, for the most part, to suppress his negative feelings.

In Session No. 59, after the incident of the film experiment, to which patient reacts with great humiliation and anger, patient's critical accusations of therapist become more ardent and reach new heights of intensity. Although therapist interprets patient's anger as not being objectively justified, he is calmly accepting of patient's criticism, and remains warm and reassuring. In the succeeding hours therapist continues to be a warm, strong, supportive, empathic, and understanding father-older brother surrogate who, however, firmly continues to expect patient to accept emancipation from him as from an "internalized brother-image." Patient reacts to the discussion of emancipation with tears and grief, which eventually gets suppressed. Therapist, although sympathetic toward such feelings, nevertheless continues to emphasize that patient give up such dependent relationships.

New or Increased Awarenesses

During this period patient acquired the following:

A. A heightened emotional awareness of his need to please therapist and be accepted and approved of by him, an increased awarness of the intensity of his feelings, both positive and negative, in relation to therapist, and of the gratification that he obtains from being dependent on others, and particularly, on therapist. Also, an increasing recognition toward the end of this period that therapist expects him to emancipate himself from therapist, with increasing sadness and anxiety at the anticipation of the expected final emancipation from therapist.

B. Beginning intellectual realization that his mother may have actually liked him more than he had always thought; also that her rejecting behavior was not specifically directed toward him but was due to her own neurotic problems.

C. Further awareness concerning his relationship to his sister and brother:

1. of his distorted view of his sister's strength and superiority;

2. of his death wish against his brother and identification of himself and his brother with his own two sons; also an increasing awareness of his identification of therapist with his brother.

D. A heightened awareness that he inhibits anger in order not to lose dependent gratification; increased understanding of the connection between his dependency strivings, hurt pride, and his overcompensatory ambitious strivings for recognition and acceptance.

E. Increased awareness of his use of sex to enhance his masculine self-esteem; and intellectual recognition of anger as a factor in his premature ejaculation.

F. Increased awareness of his use of intellectualization as a defense against experiencing strong emotion.

G. A new awareness that feelings of adequacy and inadequacy can co-exist in him.

H. Increased awareness of the relationship of his feelings of depression to guilt over rage toward members of his original family.

I. Increased awareness of his conflicting loyalties toward his mother and his wife.

Symptomatic or Behavioral Changes

A. Increasing ability to assert himself with his mother.

B. Becoming gradually firmer, more determined, and more forceful in his relationship to therapist; increasing ability to express anger to therapist.

C. Beginning ability to reveal weaknesses also to therapist with less sense of shame.

D. An increasingly realistic awareness of his relationship to his wife, mother, brother, sister, and therapist, with consequent increasing self-esteem.

As in the previous group of sessions, these changes appear to be the result of a combination of factors involving both his experience in the interpersonal relationship with therapist and the insights listed above. The psychodynamic factors involved are essentially the same as those described at the end of the previous group of sessions: shame and guilt connected with continued and repeated awareness of his immature patterns and strivings; and diminution of irrational guilt feelings associated with hostility and self-assertiveness, as a result of mere realistic evaluation of his past and present interpersonal relationships. Probable identification with therapist and incorporation of therapist's standards of mature behavior continues, as well as compliance with therapist's expectations in order to gain and maintain therapist-parent's acceptance and approval. Patient's being able in these sessions to express more overt hostility to therapist without being punished has been a corrective emotional experience. Similarly, his receiving explicit recognition for his abilities from a good and strong father figure, and receiving continued acceptance and approval from this father-older-brother figure in spite of displaying continuing dependency longings, have served to enhace his self-esteem and probably also constitute significant corrective emotional experiences for patient.

Comparison between Observers and Therapist

The sessions between 48 and 64 are encompassed by the end of the summer vacation and the two-week Thanksgiving interruption of the therapy. During this block of sessions the therapist becomes more convinced of the patient's basic dependent weakness and reacts with skepticism to this patient's ability to overcome this conflict. When he conveys some of this to the patient, the patient reacts with strong narcissistic hurt and with anger. The therapist tries to repair this by giving the patient ample reassurance about the universality of dependent needs. A major change in the therapist's views takes place toward the end of this block of sessions when he realizes that the patient's difficulty in accepting an independent role was not due to an inherent weakness but to guilt feelings about competition with the brother. Due to identification with the brother, aggression and self-assertion means self-destruction. When this becomes clear to the therapist, he expresses satisfaction and optimism about possible changes in the patient and about the outcome of the therapy. The therapist's irritability, noticed by the team in the first phase of this block of sessions, and the therapist's heightened activity toward the end of these sessions must have been due to this conflict about the therapy.

Both team and therapist agree that the therapist made major efforts to soothe the patient's hurt feelings when the therapist mentioned his dependent needs and asked him to accept them and learn to live with them. The team felt that the patient made use of his strong reaction of pain and anger and he maneuvered the therapist into giving him reassurance. The therapist agrees to some degree with this view but he also feels that he became more reassuring not due to any maneuvers on the part of the patient but to his own conviction that the pain was too great and the patient needed such reassurance. The team feels that the patient is living out a parent-child transference relationship and is avoiding bringing to the fore latent homosexual fears. The team also states that the therapist is encouraging defenses rather than uncovering them. Therapist does not go along with this formulation by the team. Team and therapist agree, on the other hand, that the patient received ample permission to express anger toward the therapist and that the patient underwent a corrective emotional experience when he expressed such feelings without being rejected by the therapist.

Both team and therapist agree that the transference is basically positive and that the patient has gone through a considerable corrective emotional experience due to his ability to express anger and has also been able to experience the therapist as a strong, giving, father-image, who has given him recognition in spite of his continuous dependency. The team and the therapist also agree about the patient's deepening intellectual insight about his hostile feelings.

During this group of sessions, the therapist has asked the patient to undergo some physiological experimentation about his feelings, namely, to view a film while being wired for physiological reactions. The patient reacted to this by conforming, but then after the test he was able to express anger toward the therapist. The team felt the patient was somewhat justified in accusing the therapist of not regarding his feelings with more understanding, while the therapist felt that the patient's reactions were exaggerated. Toward the end of this block of sessions, the patient showed considerable sadness and the team attributes this to the impending two-week interruption of the therapy, while the therapist did not consider this factor as significant enough but attributed it instead to the patient's general sadness whenever he recognizes, in therapy, the need to give up his dependent needs—on his brother in the past, on the therapist in the transference.

The team accepts the patient's good feelings as real progress, while the therapist sees these expressions of good feelings in part as progress but also as a desire to please the therapist and to continue to depend upon him. Both team and therapist agree that the ability to express negative feelings toward the therapist is considerable progress in this patient's therapy. In spite of this, the team still feels that there are more negative feelings that the patient does not express due to fear, while both team and therapist agree that the climate is favorable enough for the patient to bring out whatever negative feelings he may have toward the therapist. At one point during these sessions the team noticed irritability in the therapist and that he deliberately tried to curb this. The therapist did not mention this feeling. The reverse of this situation happened shortly afterward in another session, when the therapist felt irritated and mentioned this in the posthour dictation, while the team did not recognize this feeling.

Both therapist and team agree that the patient is undergoing both intellectual and emotional insight about his dependency conflict. The therapist stresses the fact that his interpretations have begun to penetrate emotionally. The team does not stress the emotional recognition on the part of the patient as much as the therapist does.

During this phase of the therapy, both the therapist and the team are in greater agreement about the psychodynamics of the patient's conflicts and about the transference. Also, during this phase, the therapist is becoming more aware of his own emotional participation in the therapy. This was seen by the team earlier in the therapy, possibly due to the fact that the team was not involved. The team is more aware of the therapist's conscious strategy both from direct observation and from reading the therapist's posthour dictation.

11

Therapy—Sessions 65–80

Summary of Manifest Events

Session No. 65 (11 December 1958)

Patient relates feeling good during interruption of therapy, but there was a return of tension and headaches just prior to its resumption. He relates a dream in which a sadistic husband dies, to the relief of his dependent and masochistic wife, who had been struggling to become a "mensch." In the dream the husband is revived by a "silly" student. At this point, patient is very moved and sobs. He interprets that he is the wife and that the analyst is the upsetting factor that is keeping him down, and adds that he almost cried when he realized he had death wishes toward the analyst. Therapist interprets patient's dependency-independency conflict in a variety of contexts and jokingly chides patient for not knowing whether he wants to be a man or a woman. When patient relates this to his lack of potency, therapist reassures him regarding his potency and psychological strength, stating that patient clings to his symptoms in order to cling to therapist. When patient complains about his headache and requests empirin-codeine, therapist does not grant this request for medication, but instead interprets the headache as an expression of patient's hostility toward therapist and patient's brother, due to frustration of his dependency wishes. Much intellectual discussion ensues about these psychodynamic formulations. Therapist points out patient's ambivalent

123

feelings and the hostile component that produces guilt. At this point sadness and tears are observed in patient. The session is ended early by therapist, at number 40.

Session No. 66 (15 December 1958)

This session consists of discussions about the emotional dynamics of patient's weepy feelings and his ambivalance about emancipation from brother and therapist. It also deals at length with the image of himself that he perpetuates of being dependent and weak and how this creates anger and guilt. Patient refers briefly to the "bond" he feels toward his brother and therapist, which they do not feel toward him. Thereafter the discussion emphasizes patient's wanting to feel better so he won't need any more therapy. Subsequently there is an interchange about staying sick to thwart therapist, and feeling guilty toward brother if the, patient, is well and strong. Toward the end of the session, therapist comments, "We are both groping."

Session No. 67 (18 December 1958)

The session consists largely of intellectual interchanges centering about dynamic formulations of patient's relationship with his brother, especially conflicts about emancipation, inferiority-superiority, and the need for recognition. These were interpreted as being connected with patient's headaches, anger, competitive and destructive impulses toward his brother and therapist as a brother symbol, and his identification with them; also with consequent guilt feelings, leading to a need for failure. Therapist stresses that the return to therapy reactivates these conflicts, that the Christmas vacation will provide a respite and a help, and that he must learn to live by himself. Patient agrees that when he is away from his brother and the therapist he feels more of an entity and accepts the Christmas vacation without observable negative reactions.

Session No. 68 (22 December 1958)

After some preliminary interchanges about dependency and anger, and independence and guilt, the discussions focus predominantly on patient's excessive identification with his brother, the resultant difficulty in achieving a sense of personal identity, and the effect on his self-evaluation. The impending Christmas vacation is briefly discussed, therapist again expressing his belief that it will give patient a chance to relate to himself better.

In response to a query from patient, therapist states that from the state of patient's intellectual understanding and emotional experiencing of his conflict, the therapy will probably be terminated in about two months. Patient reacts by agreeing about his improvement, laughingly indicates he wants praise, but nonverbal expressions also reveal sadness and tension. Toward the end of the session, therapist points out that the triangular situation with mother and brother no longer exists, that the problem is patient's relationship with himself, and his self-evaluation as a person separate from his brother.

Session No. 69 (4 January 1959)

Resuming therapy after the Christmas vacation, patient reports he has been symptom-free. During the first part of the session the discussion revolves around (1) patient's struggle to give up his attachment to and identification with his brother, (2) the displacement of his ambivalent feelings toward his brother onto his younger son, (3) the triangular relationship involving patient, his wife, and his brother. There is brief discussion, initiated by patient, of the "transference neurosis," and patient's struggle to separate himself from therapist as a brother substitute. This is followed by further discussions about patient's relationship with his wife and family, Patient agreeing with therapist's interpretations and explanations about how the change in his feelings toward his brother influences his other relationships. Near the end of the session, therapist states that the conflicts about the brother and mother are lessened and that material about the father needs to be dealt with, to which patient agrees.

Session No. 70 (8 January 1959)

Patient reports some tension and somewhat anxiously indicates he does not consider himself ready to terminate so soon. Patient attributes his anxiety to therapist mentioning his father, but therapist interprets that patient uses the father as a justification to prolong therapy. Patient sighs and reports a dream in which a gangster is beating up patient's brother, then to his surprise his father comes in banged up, and the brother disappears. The rest of the session consists of an attempt to understand the dream and to reconstruct patient's relationship with his father. During this discussion patient feels tense and anxious.

Session No. 71 (12 January 1959)

Therapist and patient cooperatively continue the work of trying to clarify the psychodynamics of patient's relationship with his father and the dream about the father. In response to patient's associations about his past experiences with father, therapist confidently, repeatedly, and actively presents his interpretations that patient was afraid to identify with the weak father, and so substituted the brother, whom he had to make strong. Therapist explains patient's anxious reaction to the discussion of the father during the previous session on this basis. Patient agrees with therapist's interpretations and explanations, and both therapist and patient are visibly pleased and satisfied.

Session No. 72 (15 January 1959)

During the first part of the session, patient relates several current reality episodes involving brother figures, and therapist uses them to interpret patient's ambivalent wishes to "defeat" and at the same time to "build up" brothers. Patient has difficulty remembering the details of the previous session, is reminded of them by therapist, who then elaborates at considerable length his interpretations that patient fears letting go of his dependency on brother and turning to the father, who appeared weak. An interchange centering around these interpretations then follows, with patient apparently developing awareness of these patterns in his interaction with several brother figures.

Session No. 73 (18 January 1959)

Patient states that he had two new insights: one that he fears losing his wife's love as he feared losing mother's; the other that he clings to his dependency on his brother because of a positive identification with his brother's strength, which he fears losing. Therapist leads patient back to the discussion of his relationship with his father and points out that patient has been avoiding it during the past two sessions. This leads into a detailed animated and cooperative discussion concerning patient's disappointment in, and resentment toward, his father for "letting mother down"; how patient was then expected to take the role of a father-substitute; and how he protected himself against his demanding mother by building up his brother as a father-surrogate instead. Patient verbalizes intensely sad feelings when he talks of "letting go of brother." Therapist concludes the session with the statement that they will continue "plodding on" in the next session.

Session No. 74 (22 January 1959)

Patient reproaches therapist for his use of the word *plodding*, and therapist's defending it as a mere "facon de parler." Patient and therapist then cooperatively continue the discussion of patient's feelings concerning his delegating the father-surrogate role to his brother. In the middle of the session, therapist excuses himself and leaves the room for three minutes. On his return patient resumes talking as if nothing had happened. After a discussion of patient's tendency to avoid responsibility in relationship to his wife, just as he previously did with mother, therapist laughingly comments that patient could write a book entitled "How I Was Castrated by My Mother," and then terminates the session about fifteen minutes early. Patient questions this mildly but does not press the point.

Session No. 75 (26 January 1959)

Patient reports feeling depressed since the previous session, and attributes it to a reaction to therapist's joke about patient's having been "castrated" by his mother. The discussion that ensues leads into patient's feelings about, and identification with, his "weak" father. Therapist endeavors to soften the narcissistic blow of this identification by being warm, supportive, and encouraging and by minimizing patient's view of his father's supposed weakness.

Session No. 76 (29 January 1959)

Patient continues his discussion of his identification with the depreciated father, but with less anxiety. He also discusses his fear of women, which he traces back to his fear of his "man-eating" mother. He then goes into an account of the family circumstances at the time of his birth that led to his mother's favoring his brother over him. The interaction between therapist and patient continues to be an active and cooperative one, with patient appearing noticeably less ingratiating and submissive and more mature in his relationship with therapist.

Session No. 77 (2 February 1959)

In this session patient's behavior returns regressively to that of the complaining, helpless, dependent little boy, as he discusses a recurrence of anxiety that he has experienced in the last few days. In the course of the ensuing discussion this anxiety is attributed to his changing concepts about his mother, father, and brother, and his guilt and fear of success in connection with a possible promotion on his job. Therapist responds to patient's feelings with warmth, encouragement, and reassurance that patient can function at a mature masculine level.

Session No. 78 (5 February 1959)

Patient is euphoric as he reports that the promotion has taken place. The discussion then deals with patient's reactions to his promotion, and the importance of guarding against his former tendency to push other people ahead of him so that he could justify his weak self-image and his wish to lean on others. The interaction between patient and therapist is once again free, active, warm, and at a mature level.

Session No. 79 (9 February 1959)

Patient reports feelings of tension and depression since the previous session. He attributes this to feeling guilty toward both his father and brother because of the success implicit in his recent promotion. An active and animated discussion then ensues between patient and therapist about these guilt feelings, and their relationship to competitive and aggressive attitudes toward father and brother. Therapist confronts patient reassuringly with the fact that there is no realistic basis for his guilt, and toward the end of the session patient reports that his tension has left him and he is feeling much better.

Session No. 80 (13 February 1959)

Patient reports smilingly that he has been very upset for the past two days, but that he has managed to pull out of it himself. What had happened was that he had been told that his promotion would have to be postponed for certain administrative reasons. The ensuing discussion deals with his overreaction to this situation and the reasons for it. The therapist is warm, giving, supportive, and reassuring to patient, who in turns gives the impression that he is trying to please therapist by demonstrating his ability to surmount a frustrating situation without being crushed by it.

Therapist-Patient Interaction

In Session No. 65 patient and therapist work together in a warm, friendly, cooperative way, predominantly engaged in a lively and emotionally tinged discussion about the dream, and about dependency-independency, hostility, guilt, and fear. Patient's longings for love from brother and analyst, and the sadness connected with these frustrated longings are observed in his behavior, but are not verbalized. Therapist's interventions reveal his implicit wish for patient to become "emancipated and independent." He jokingly chides patient for not knowing whether he wants to be "a man or a woman."

Session No. 66 is essentially like Session No. 65 except that patient is more than usually independent, disagreeing with therapist several times, with therapist remaining friendly and accepting. During the last part of the session, which seems confusing, therapist with an unusual degree of humility, comments, "we are both groping."

In Session No. 67, therapist and patient are engaged in the task of achieving understanding about patient's relationship with brother in a mutually friendly cooperative manner, with therapist giving many psychodynamic explanations and patient predominantly agreeing with and confirming therapist's interpretations. Patient is overtly accepting of therapist's attitude that a Christmas vacation is good for him, and that he should strive to become independent of the brother, of the therapist, and of the therapy, but sighs, suggesting some deeper unhappy feelings.

In the following session, therapist encourages patient to "separate" from brother and from therapist, to establish his own "identity" and self-evaluations, and emphasizes patient's capacity to accomplish this. Patient responds positively to this and there is an observable mobilization of his mature masculine strivings. Patient and therapist continue to work cooperatively as equals. In Session No. 69 therapist appears to be satisfied with patient's attitudes and insights, and to be consistently encouraging and supportive. There is no direct verbal expression of patient's feelings, but according to one observer the nonverbal expression reveals some underlying sadness and tension, presumably connected with the discussions of psychological separation from brother and the implied actual separation from therapist.

In Sessions No. 70 and No. 71 therapist and patient attempt to understand the dream and the complexities of patient's past relationship with his father. Therapist's attitude is kindly, warm, understanding, and at one point he frankly admits that he is not sure of the interpretation and that patient's theory about the dream may be more correct. Patient briefly reveals some anxiety and concern as a reaction to therapist's evident intentions about termination in the near future and therapist's emphasis on patient's improved functioning and insights.

In Session No. 72, therapist and patient appear to get satisfaction from the predominantly intellectual interchanges and the understandings that are being achieved. During the past week, patient's conscious concern about separation and termination has apparently subsided and patient appears to be enjoying the relationship with therapist, who had been consistently friendly and actively giving and helpful with his interpretations and explanations. Therapist has also been consistently treating patient as an equal and even admitting that patient's theories were more correct than therapist's on several occasions. Patient even permits himself a little affectionate teasing, with mildly competitive aggressive undertones, which therapist accepts in a friendly way. This is like a good father and adolescent-son relationship in which son accepts his subordinate role with a superior, kindly, helpful father whose knowledge and wisdom he respects, from whom he receives psychological help, and to whom he expresses his rivalry in mild affectionate teasing that the father is able to accept tolerantly. It is apparent that the therapist's attitude toward patient has become more tolerant and accepting as patient's behavior has become less demanding and dependent.

In Sessions No. 73 and No. 74 therapist continues to be friendly, warm, helping in the work. At one point, patient unconsciously attempts to maintain the fantasy of therapist as the omniscient parent, but therapist thwarts this by giving patient equal credit for unraveling his conflicts. Patient and therapist work together as equals, with mutual satisfaction despite some emotionally disturbing discussions. Patient reacts with signs of gratification when therapist appears satisfied and encouraging about his "progress" in achieving insights, and is disappointed when he interprets therapist's attitude as one of dissatisfaction, as when therapist used the words "plodding along." Therapist states in his work sheet that he is very pleased "that the total picture becomes clearer." When therapist terminates Session No. 74 at thirty-four minutes, patient protests mildly but then accepts the situation with little observable evidence of strong feelings.

In Session No. 75 therapist seems to react to patient's sad, anxious state by being particularly gentle, kindly, and supportive, attempting to restore patient's self-regard, which has greatly diminished as a reaction to discussions about being "castrated" by mother, and by therapist's interpretations that patient is a similar kind of husband, as his "weak" father. Therapist comments on patient's sadness, and evidently to neutralize this reaction, therapist suggests that father was not so weak.

In Session No. 76, the relationship between therapist and patient continues to be an active and cooperative one as man to man. The submissive and ingratiating behavior of patient is noticeably lessened. Therapist is friendly and supportive and, according to the statements in his work sheet, attempts to foster patient's identification with him as a man who can laugh at, not be frightened by, aggressive women. This seems to be a reaction of therapist to patient's fear of his aggressive mother. Therapist continues to emphasize the father's strengths.

In the next session patient is somewhat regressed and again behaves like a whining helpless dependent child, as a reaction to the proferred promotion in his work. Therapist emphasizes in his interpretations that patient cannot permit himself to feel strong and well and be successful because of guilt feelings associated with his depreciation of his father. Therapist in a warm and reassuring manner emphasizes that patient has had illusions about both himself and his father being weak, thus implying that patient is really strong and encouraging him to assume the masculine role.

In Session No. 78 patient's mood is euphoric as he reports that the promotion has taken place. Therapist continues his efforts to help patient change his former weak self-image to a more realistic, adequate one. Therapist's attitude toward patient is a warm and approving one. He appears to be pleased with patient's more mature behavior, his promotion, his reaction to it, and to his progress in the treatment. He indicates his confidence in patient's capacities. Patient appears pleased to be so valued and approved of by this idealized analyst-parent. Therapist's effort to encourage patient's identification with him is indicated by his repeated use of the word *we*.

In the following session patient reports feeling tense and depressed since the previous session. Patient and therapist attribute this to guilt feelings connected with his promotion, and recognition of his superiority over his brother and father. It is also possible that the tension and depressed feelings are partly a reaction to his success and the focusing on his abilities, which threatens his longing for passive-dependent position. The therapist reconstructs in detail patient's psychodynamics (in his work sheet therapist states that this may have been for the benefit of a visiting colleague who was observing). At the same time he is friendly and accepting and repeatedly reassures patient that he has nothing realistically to feel guilty about, as he has done nothing to damage his brother or father. He also gives reassuring explanations about patient's fears, following which patient's tension subsides. Therapist continues to reveal his wish for patient to give up what therapist laughingly refers to as his "schmo" self-image.

In Session No. 80 the main feature in the interaction is patient's living out the role of the son, proudly displaying to therapist-parent his success in using insights and self-control to master the anxiety and depression with which he reacted to news about postponement of his promotion, and to resist the temptation to lean on therapist by telephoning him. Therapist, according to his work sheet, is aware of patient's wishes for praise and recognition. He does not gratify them directly, but, while discussing patient's reactions, conflicts, and motivations he indirectly does so by reassuring patient about his worth and adequacy, and about his deserving and getting his promotion.

Therapeutic Experience of the Patient

In the Interpersonal Relationship

The warm, supportive, empathic, and encouraging behavior of therapist continues consistently throughout this period. At the same time, however, therapist is firm in refusing patient's request for medication (Session No. 65). Therapist continues to reveal to patient, both implicitly and explicitly, his desire to see him function on his own; shows trust and confidence in patient's strength and ability to do so; and his satisfaction with patient's progress and insights reveals itself on a number of occasions. Therapist no longer acts like the omniscient and omnipotent parent, but rather like a helpful, kindly, and understanding father-brother surrogate and "partner." On one occasion (Session No. 66) when the material becomes rather confusing, therapist is able to confess, "We're both groping today"; and on another occasion (Session No. 73), when patient unconsciously attempts to reinstitute the fantasy of therapist as the omniscient parent, therapist thwarts this by giving patient equal credit for the unraveling of his conflicts.

Presumably in response to this experience with therapist, patient gradually relates to therapist more and more maturely and confidently, as an equal. He asserts himself more aggressively, is able to contradict therapist repeatedly, to chide him at times for inadequate interpretations, and even to compete with him by offering what he considers more adequate ones.

On two occasions, during this period, however, patient regresses. In Session No. 75, after a previous session in which therapist had identified patient with his weak and depreciated father, and has also terminated the session after only thirty-four minutes, patient reverted to the behavior of a guilty, apprehensive boy; but under therapist's particularly gentle and reassuring behavior was able by the end of the session to recover some of his self-esteem and to express anger toward therapist. In Session No. 77, possibly in reaction to guilt feelings toward his brother and father resulting from his job promotion, patient reverts to his earlier patterns of the whining, complaining, helpless, dependent, little boy. Therapist again, however, is warm, reassuring, and understanding; encourages patient to assume the masculine role; and indicates that he is strong enough to do so. In the remaining three sessions of this period, patient resumes his more mature relationship to therapist. On a number of occasions during this period the question of termination arises. Therapist does not focus upon it, however, and the inference is that patient's reactions to termination and separation are thus covertly discouraged.

New or Increased Awareness

During this period patient acquired the following:

A. A heightened awareness of his ambivalent feeling toward therapist; namely his desire to cling to and lean on therapist, and his desire to get rid of him as a threat to his independence and masculinity. Also a recognition that similar feelings exist in relationship to his brother.

B. Some intellectual awareness that his receptive, dependent wishes have a "feminine" as well as a little-child quality, and that he feels small and weak when these are operating.

C. Intellectual and emotional recognition of guilt feelings associated with becoming independent of brother and therapist, and with feeling psychologically stronger than his brother; also guilt associated with successes in life. Also of fantasies that therapist and brother need him and will collapse if he leaves them.

D. A heightened awareness of the intensity of his identification with his brother, and of guilt about acquiring an identity separate from brother.

E. Increasing awareness, both intellectually and emotionally, of his fear of being identified with his weak, depreciated father, and of how he built up the image of a strong brother as a compensatory defense; and of his ambivalent, competitive, and masochistic relationships with brother and various brother-surrogates.

F. A new awareness, both cognitive and emotional, of the significance of father's weakness in his childhood; of how mother turned to his brother and him to be the men in her life, and how patient, fearing that mother would "destroy" him as she did father, then delegated the father role to his brother. At the same time, a new awareness of his own childhood hostility to father, of his wishes to get rid of him, and consequently of an ambivalent wish to replace father in the relationship with mother.

G. A heightened awareness of the relationship between these historical events and his developing sexual impotence when his wife began to make demands on him.

H. A reappraisal of father's qualities and a gradual recognition that his childhood picture of him was a distorted one, and that father was actually a stronger and more worthwhile person who could be respected and liked; also guilt associated with the new awareness of the extent to which he had unjustifiably rejected his father.

I. Increasing awareness of the connection between his fear of women and his childhood fear of his aggressive mother.

J. Increasing awareness, both cognitive and emotional, that his previous image of himself as weak is not valid, and of his fears of giving up this depreciated self-image as he is gradually replacing it with a more masculine and self-accepting one.

K. Increased differentiation between mother and wife.

Symptomatic or Behavioral Changes

During this period all observers agreed that patient showed:

A. more maturity and self-assertiveness in his relationship to therapist as well as in his interpersonal relationships outside of therapy;

B. diminution of his former masochistic tendencies toward various brother-surrogates with whom he comes into contact;

C. a changing self-image in the direction of increased masculinity, with increase in self-confidence;

D. a more accepting and friendly relationship with his father.

In evaluating the basis for these changes the conclusion again seems warranted that they are the result of a combination of factors involving the interpersonal transaction with therapist, and the insights listed above. Some of the significant psychodynamic factors that seem to be involved are as follows:

A. Continued diminution of irrational guilt feelings associated with aggressiveness and self-assertiveness, as a result of

  1. More realistic evaluation of his past and present interpersonal relationships.

  2. Repeated and continued corrective emotional experiences involving his ability to contradict, challenge, tease, and express aggressive feelings to therapist and other persons without experiencing retaliation or counterhostility; also his experiencing therapist as a consistently warm, supportive, understanding and encouraging father-surrogate, who is not only no longer deprecating or controlling, but who also expresses confidence in patient's strength and ability.

B. Continued identification with therapist and incorporation of therapist's standards of mature behavior, as well as unconscious compliance with therapist's expectations in order to gain and maintain therapist-parent's approval; with probable suppression and repression of his passive-dependent strivings. A significant corollary of this is the loosening of patient's identification with the distorted image of a weak and disparaged father, and a new awareness of his father's actual strengths.

C. A loosening of his identification with his brother, and an increasing sense of his own separate identity.

Comparison between Observers and Therapist

The therapist's report consists predominantly of descriptions of the working out of the psychodynamics of the patient's attitudes and patterns in his present interpersonal relationships, including those with the therapist, and reconstructing their development in the childhood family relationships. The therapist describes his own working out of the dynamic formulations; the new awarenesses of the patient during the course of the discussions; and the therapist's communications about the patient's internal patterns, conflicts, solutions, motivations, etc., in the past and in the present. The therapist makes a number of referencs to the therapist-patient interaction. In one summary he states that the "patient is discovering that by frustrating the therapist—by clinging to his dependency needs—he can provoke him into becoming overactive, which he passively enjoys." He also mentions identification with the therapist, and considers it an attempt to overcome dependency. On another occasion the therapist states that the "transference is still passive-dependent, but the therapist expects the patient will reexperience the traumatic feeling about father weakness which caused him to make a strong father figure out of his brother; he clung to this idea which is now being destroyed. The therapist expects that he will cling equally strongly to the analyst's image as an omnipotent figure." The therapist also makes a number of references to his encouraging the patient to express anger, which the therapist considers a corrective emotional experience. He also refers to the patient's "trend toward seeking reconciliation with the therapist for expressing his anger."

The team is, in general, in agreement with the therapist regarding the content of the intellectual-cognitive insights being acquired by the patient. Although the team regards the emotional component to be present in some of the insights, they describe it less than does the therapist. Also, the team sees much more compliance in some of the "insights" than does the therapist.

As in previous blocks of hours, the team describes the ongoing therapist-patient interaction in much greater detail and more consistently, but the therapist is making more references to the therapist-patient interpersonal relationship than formerly. The team emphasizes much more than does the therapist the living out in the transference of the son role by the patient, especially his attempts to modify his behavior and attitudes in the direction of the covert wishes and the model of maturity presented to him by the therapist. Both team and therapist are in agreement about the patient's experience in expressing anger and asserting himself with the therapist without encountering retaliation. Both consider this a corrective emotional experience that decreases the patient's fear of aggression and permits the further development of healthy aggression. The team puts greater emphasis on the change in the therapist's attitude and its effect than does the therapist.

The team and the therapist have some difference in their appraisal of the fate of the patient's passive-dependent strivings and longings for love and intimacy with the therapist and with the brother. The therapist almost explicitly communicates his wish for patient to give them up. He realizes that the patient cannot do this completely, and also makes this explicit. From his descriptions he seems to believe that the patient is partially "giving them up." The team, in contrast, infers that they are being largely suppressed and repressed, motivated by the patient's unconscious desire to conform to the therapist's expectations, and his own masculine ideal. The team also stresses identification with the therapist by the patient as an important factor responsible for the change in the patient's behavior.

12

Therapy—Sessions 81–98

Summary of Manifest Events

Session No. 81 (16 February 1959)

Patient reports with considerable emotion conflicts and anxieties associated with his growing awareness of the separate identities of his son, his brother, and himself and listens carefully to therapist's extensive discussion about patient's conflicts in relation to his brother, and his anxiety about becoming an individual on his own and a father to his children. Patient also reports anxieties about his promotion following a change in the administration and is given reassurances by therapist. There is some exploration of patient's inner conflict connected with his fellow workers and his superiors, in order to ascertain whether or not his previous self-defeating tendencies are operating.

Session No. 82 (19 February 1959)

Although patient's anxiety about his job situation is much less, therapist appears to have considerable concern that patient's self-defeating attitudes and that his wish to avoid the authoritative father role might be lived out and so damage his advancement in his organization. He repeatedly interprets patient's wish to avoid the father role and its various manifestations in his important interpersonal relationships. He also confronts patient with the tendency to live out these neurotic patterns. There is also some interspersed discussion about the dynamics of patient's relationship with his younger sister, including references to hostile competitive and sadistically tinged sexual feelings.

Session No. 83 (23 February 1959)

Patient reports a nightmare of which the essential features are as follows: "I was pursued by 'a thing' and was going around in circles. A man repairing the streets was annoyed at me. I was afraid to go back because the repairman might be annoyed, so I felt wedged in. The sinister looking repairman opened a gate for me and the 'thing' swooped down on me and I started screeching." Therapist relates the dream to patient's fear of his repressed hostility to his sister, and then elaborates on the genetic dynamic development of patient's repressed hostile and sexual feelings toward his sister, the associated guilt, the relation of this to the dynamics of his political views and the displacement of hostility onto his wife. Patient reveals considerable emotional disturbance during the session, to which therapist reacts with a warm supportive reassuring manner, frequently accompanying the disturbing interpretations and confrontations with warm kindly chuckling. Therapist emphasizes that although patient is getting much understanding about his early relationships, it is necessary still to clarify the relationships with his father and with therapist.

Session No. 84 (26 February 1959)

Patient reports feeling "great" because he thinks he is at the "end of his neurosis," and that he is enjoying successful intercourse without the former sadistic fantasies. Therapist and patient agree that the end of therapy is near, but that patient still has to work through his feelings toward his father.

With a high level of mutual warmth, friendliness, and frequent spontaneous laughter, the interchanges then focus mainly on patient's feelings toward his father and therapist. With active encouragement from therapist, patient, somewhat hesitantly and anxiously, admits deeper fears that both men will turn on him and throw him out. In response to therapist's direct queries, patient admits thoughts about therapist not caring about him, and fears of trusting his father and therapist, but immediately adds that he is convinced that therapist is warm and kind and that he thinks well of patient as a worthy person. Therapist, actively and in a kindly, empathic way, makes the interpretation that hostile and aggressive wishes to replace both father and therapist are responsible for his fears of hostility from them and cause him to retreat to a passive role. Patient, although nonverbal expressions revealed some feelings of embarrassment, sadness, and tension, cooperatively brings out some confirmatory material.

Session No. 85 (2 March 1959)

Patient reports that he has reacted to the new insights about his father by feeling emotionally upset. There is a considerable amount of intellectualizing about the conflicts in relation to father and therapist. With the help of therapist's supportive kindness and persistent pressure from therapist to face his hostile feelings, patient experiences and expresses his fears of therapist's possible anger and cruelty, and his intense desire to keep therapist's approval, especially as he considers therapist the only father figure who has given him a lot of approval and "makes him feel good about himself." With therapist constantly using the technique of warmly laughing to protect patient's easily disturbed self-esteem, the discussion continues about patient's feelings of weakness, his repressed wishes to replace the father and therapist, the resulting loss of the dependent role, the loneliness associated with becoming an independent father himself, and the guilt and fears of retaliation.

Session No. 86 (5 March 1959)

Throughout the session there is much interchange about patient's conflictual feelings toward therapist, his wish to lean on therapist, and wishes to get rid of and replace him. These attitudes are compared to similar childhood feelings about replacing father with mother. Therapist actively presents to patient his concept of the mature person who no longer is involved with this type of rivalry and forcefully stresses the importance of patient recognizing and working with his rivalrous and destructive feelings and channelizing his aggressions into creative and productive activity. Patient has considerable tension during these discussions and expresses feelings of guilt and sadness. The sadness is interpreted as a reaction to losing the father figure.

Session No. 87 (12 March 1959)

Following patient's complaining about therapist having cancelled the previous appointment, about anxiety and premature ejaculations, and about his tension at staff meetings, there are largely intellectual interchanges dealing mainly with the conflict between patient's competitive wishes to displace father figures, including his brother, and his wish to retain and lean on them. Therapist's comments reveal his intention to terminate therapy and patient reacts by indicating his fears and reluctance. Therapist repeatedly ascribes patient's anxieties and symptoms, including the recurrence of premature ejaculations, to an unconscious wish to continue therapy and the dependent relationship with therapist; to patient's fears of being independent and alone; and to fantasies that successful competition with the father is equivalent to destruction of him. He also takes the position that patient will have to accept the anxiety that therapist claims goes along with assuming a new independent role.

Session No. 88 (16 March 1959)

Patient expresses conscious anxiety about the separation from therapist and therapy, and reports a dream in which he was going back and forth between his former group therapist and the present therapist. The subsequent interchanges revolve around interruption or termination of therapy and patient's wish to continue the dependent relationship with therapist as a parental figure. Therapist explicitly expresses his attitude that patient has reached a sufficient level of maturity, that his fears and wish to maintain this dependent relationship are residues from childhood and that patient will now resolve this in life and not in the therapy. Firmly, but in a supportive and reassuring way, he opposes patient's desire to continue in the therapy situation and thus hold on to therapist. He informs patient that the sessions will be reduced to once a week in the near future, and that there will be a follow-up session one year after termination. Patient's overt reaction appears to be an understanding and accepting one.

Session No. 89 (19 March 1959)

Patient begins by asking therapist "how are you doing" and then asks questions about various physical symptoms of his own. In response to therapist's inquiry about this "bombardment" of questions, patient verbalizes a wish for someone to look after him and a wish to not lose therapist. Patient and therapist then agree on the formulation that patient is regressively reacting to the knowledge that he no longer needs the therapist by wanting to cling to therapist as a substitute father. Exploration of patient's initial inquiry about therapist's health elicits the information that patient is feeling more mature, more like a colleague, in fact, a little cocky. The mechanics of tapering off the sessions and terminating therapy are then discussed. Despite his wish not to give up the therapy and therapist, patient's attitude about the imminent termination is a cooperative and accepting one. Following this he expresses his pleasure that through his therapy he has made a contribution to the research.

Session No. 90 (23 March 1959)

Patient reports increased anxiety, which he attributes to a series of events over the weekend involving psychiatric difficulties in a number of people he knows. He feels he has a tendency to over-identify with others. He then discusses a new job possibility but decides he would rather stay where he is. Next, he describes a number of events that reveal his increased security in dealing with his wife, his son, and his mother. Therapist is unusually quiet this session and patient finally comments on this. Therapist gives no explanation and patient seems to become slightly apprehensive. He states that he is becoming anxious because of the approaching termination and therapist nods his assent, then terminates the session ten minutes early, looking rather tired.

Session No. 91 (26 March 1959)

Patient reports he has been feeling more tranquil and has had satisfactory intercourse despite some premature ejaculation. A somewhat intellectual discussion ensues about techniques and psychodynamics of termination. Therapist reassures patient that he can expect his improvement to continue after termination and that there will be a follow-up interview after one year. Patient reports that he still has some obsessive thoughts about his younger son, and a discussion follows about the relationship between this symptom and his struggle to achieve a separate identity from his brother. Therapist compares termination of therapy with a swimming teacher's method of gradually letting go of the rope that ties the student to him. Patient then laughingly asks therapist if he had been correct the previous session in analyzing therapist's silence as a deliberate termination strategy. Therapist explains that he had actually been very fatigued. Termination is again animatedly discussed, with therapist reassuring patient about the ultimate results of therapy, emphasizing that patient's neurotic dependency needs are much diminished. Patient accepts this appraisal. Therapist then states that patient's therapeutic experience was as good as if he'd had four to five times a week of psychoanalysis for four to five years and that "there will be some residues, but after all, everybody has them."

Session No. 92 (2 April 1959)

Patient is now on a once-a-week schedule. He reports markedly increased anxiety during the past week, at times so intense that he had a fear of disintegrating. Therapist, laughing gently, interprets this as an effort on the part of patient to threaten therapist "to keep the therapy going," and reassures patient that he won't disintegrate. The rest of the session consists of an elaboration of this theme, with parallels being drawn between patient's anxiety and anger at therapist's leaving him and his earlier anxiety and anger at his brother when the latter left him. Patient expresses the wish to set the time for termination himself. Therapist and patient agree that this has the purpose of saving patient's pride. By the end of the session, patient's tensions have subsided markedly, and he terminates the session himself, with a humorous comment on his "calling the time."

Session No. 93 (9 April 1959)

Patient reports continued anxiety, which he relates intellectually to the approaching termination. In spite of this, however, he states that his sexual performance is "pretty good" and that he is doing very competent work on his job. Most of the session consists of efforts on the part of therapist to have patient identify and express his feelings about termination, but patient insists he cannot do so. Therapist stresses that patient must be having feelings both of anger and envy and relates these feelings to those that patient had when his brother left him after the war. Patient tends to reject these interpretations but therapist forcefully insists on them and urges patient again and again to make an effort to let his feelings out. He states that patient really wishes to be his equal and links this with similar feelings on patient's part toward his superior. Patient finally admits that this may be so, but that this is realistically impossible in both instances. Therapist suggests that patient should neverthe-less "follow this thought and play with the idea" of competition and hostility toward therapist.

Session No. 94 (16 April 1959)

Patient asks therapist if he is going to a forthcoming convention and therapist states that he is. Patient then reports feeling better in the past several days. He describes an incident of violent rage at his wife for wanting to visit her father, and also continued obses-sions concerning the parentage of his younger son. Therapist inter-prets patient's rage at his wife as a displacement of his anger at being deserted by the therapist-father in therapy. The obsessions about his son are discussed in terms of his reluctance to accept his own separate identity and his role as a father. Patient then reports a dream in which a man exchanges patient's own nice and shiny car for an identical model that is more worn, but finally helps patient get his own back. Patient interprets the dream himself as having to do with his trying to find his own individuality, separate from his brother. Therapist agrees and stresses that patient is the better and the stronger of the two. He states that this seems like a resolution dream. Patient has an impulse to make this the last session, but therapist states that he would like to see patient again after the three-week convention interruption.

Session No. 95 (7 May 1959)

Patient reports an alternation of relapses, including an episode of impotence, and improvements during the three-week interruption. Therapist points out that patient feels good after interrupting therapy, but anxious and depressed on resuming it. This leads to discussion about symbiotic relationships, dependency, rivalry, hostility, and guilt toward therapist and the relationship of these feelings to earlier feelings toward his brother. On several occasions patient forthrightly rejects therapist's interpretations and offers others of his own, which therapist accepts. Therapist focuses on patient's wish to be the one who terminates the therapy, and speculates that there is a feeling of victory over therapist with a wish for revenge (to make therapist "feel bad") and consequent guilt connected with these feelings. Patient laughingly agrees that it's not enough for him to be successful, he has to "push therapist's face in the mud" in the process. Therapist laughingly reassures patient that he "will go on working very nicely," and patient joins in the laughter with apparent relief. Patient then reports that his mother is angry at his brother's wife because their son has been having emotional difficulties. Therapist suggests that this may be a displacement of mother's disappointment at patient's brother onto the brother's son. Patient confirms this and expresses amazement and admiration at therapist's "cleverness."

Session No. 96 (14 May 1959)

Patient reports continued feelings of tension and depression, which he and therapist both attribute to the approaching termination. Patient indicates that there is still a transference connection between his brother and therapist in his mind. Patient then reports an upsetting experience at his place of work, where a co-worker did what patient considered something unprofessional to him. Patient became angry, and reported it to his superior. When the colleague was about to be fired, however, patient intervened on his behalf and afterwards felt depressed. Therapist interprets this as being due to guilt at victory over a brother-competitor, and then suggests that termination also means to patient a kind of victory over therapist, with guilt at emancipating himself from the therapist-brother. Patient then reports that his mother seems to be favoring him over his brother lately, and therapist re-emphasizes patient's guilt at his victory. Therapist goes into a fairly lengthy exposition of the relationship between patient's competitive, hostile feelings, and his consequent guilt and self-defeating tendencies. He indicates how this has operated in patient's past with his brother, as well as in his work situation, and now in the therapeutic situation. In response to patient's question, therapist states that patient's "prognosis" is good. At the end he indicates that termination is now up to patient. Patient replies that he would like to see therapist two or three more times.

Session No. 97 (21 May 1959)

After stating that he has been feeling all right, patient reports his realization that cycles of feeling well have been alternating with other cycles during which his old feelings of weakness, anger, guilt, and self-punishment still manifest themselves; and that all the things discussed and worked out in therapy are falling into place. Therapist quietly reassures patient that he is proving to himself that he can be his own analyst now and that he is now ready to be on his own. Patient reports that his superiors and co-workers have noticed a great improvement in him in the past year. Therapist indicates that patient can expect even greater improvement after he has terminated therapy, since therapy itself is a kind of artificial stress situation. Patient reacts with expressions of pleasure. Therapist again cautions patient not to expect to function "100 percent" but expresses confidence that patient will be able to "control his life situation.'' Both agree to make the next session, in two weeks, the final one. Patient would have liked to terminate therapy today but therapist suggests they have one more session. Patient seems calm and expresses confidence in his ability to terminate therapy.

Session No. 98 (4 June 1959)

Patient smilingly presents therapist with a gift for the "crew" and states that he has been feeling very well. He reports a dream in which he is being drafted into the army again but not being shipped too far from home. He awoke feeling lonely and sad. He recognizes the dream's relationship to the ending of therapy and interprets its various implications himself. He happily describes his improved relationships with his wife, children, and in-laws. During the balance of the session, therapist gently probes into various areas of patient's functioning in an admitted effort to see whether patient's improvement is genuine or just "play-acting." Patient firmly defends his progress as genuine, and therapist finally states that he is fully convinced that patient's gains are solid. He wishes patient good luck and states that he will see him again in one year, but leaves the door open for patient to call him or write to him earlier if he feels the need to do so. Patient expresses gratitude, to which therapist replies by saying he has learned as much from patient as patient has from him. Patient leaves, quite moved.

Therapist-Patient Interaction

In general the warm, supportive, empathic, and encouraging behavior of therapist continues. At the same time therapist continues to indicate that he expects patient to assume the independent mature role and separate from the therapy and from therapist. Although patient has partially conscious wishes to remain with the therapist-parent and reacts to the imminent termination with anxiety and sadness, he accepts as valid therapist's appraisal of his ability to be independent. In accord with therapist's explicit expectations, patient strives to achieve this goal and to tolerate the emotions associated with the separation.

In Session No. 82, therapist cautions patient not to live out his self-defeating attitude, which therapist attributes to his wish to avoid the adult father role, and thus jeopardize his promotion. In Session No. 84, therapist and patient agree that the end of therapy is near, and in a mutually cooperative friendly way, explore patient's feelings and conflicts. Therapist deals with patient's anxiety reaction to the interpretations about hostility and rivalry with father and therapist by providing considerable support and reassurance, and then in Session No. 86 communicates his expectation that patient will become a mature person who channels his childhood rivalries and aggressions into creative and productive activity. Although expressing agreement, patient reacts with anxiety, especially when, in Session No. 87, therapist's intention to terminate therapy soon becomes evident. During this and subsequent sessions, therapist is understanding and empathic about patient's anxiety, but firmly indicates that he expects patient to accept the anxieties that go along with assuming a new independent role, and reassures patient that he has reached a sufficient level of maturity and will be able to resolve these childhood residues.

During Sessions Nos. 89, 90, and 91, patient's overt attitude about his improvement and termination is an accepting and cooperative one, and his behavior with therapist is more like that of an equal, but a covert struggle goes on between therapist and patient about termination. In Session No. 92, patient's new complaints of increased anxiety and fears of disintegrating are countered by therapist with interpretations that patient is trying unconsciously to threaten therapist. Patient evidently realizes that therapist intends to continue with the plans for termination, accepts this as inevitable, and asks to set the time for himself.

Following this, patient succeeds again in suppressing his feelings about termination and in Session No. 93 therapist's attempt to get him to express them are unsuccessful. That repressed anger at therapist is present is revealed and interpreted when patient reports in Session No. 94 an incident of unjustified violent rage at his wife, and when he expresses the wish to make this the last session. Therapist opposes this and arranges for an appointment in three weeks. During the next few weeks, patient intermittently experiences some depressive feelings and some anxiety and has an episode of impotence. In the 95th session, therapist is accepting and permissive toward patient's assertive desire to decide the termination date independently and about patient's possible revenge wishes toward therapist. Patient reacts with observable relief and becomes cheerful.

In Session No. 96, patient continues to behave in a more independent self-reliant way. In Session No. 97 patient agrees that he does not need therapist anymore, finds this reassuring, feels ready to terminate, and emphasizes the improvements in his functioning. Therapist supportively and reassuringly joins in and also emphasizes patient's improvements and insights and his confidence in patient's future functioning, to which patient reacts with overt pleasure and gratification.

Two weeks later in the final session, No. 98, patient reports some sadness about leaving therapy, and that the knowledge that therapist will be close by and available if he needs him is reassuring. He expresses his gratitude by smilingly presenting therapist with a gift for the "crew," and stoutly defending the genuineness of his improvements when therapist questions them in order to be certain that patient is actually "ripe" for termination (therapist's work sheet). Therapist then conveys to patient that he is convinced that patient's improvements are genuine, and both therapist and patient express confidence in patient's ability to handle whatever life has in store for him. Therapist wishes patient good luck, states that he will see him in a year, and gives him permission to call or write if he feels the need for help. When patient verbalizes his gratitude and thanks for the therapy, therapist warmly states he has learned as much from patient as patient has from him.

At the end of the session when patient and therapist shake hands, patient is visibly moved. Therapist responds to patient with warm feelings (therapist's work sheet) connected with his satisfaction with patient's efforts and improvement and describes feelings of respect for patient's "integrity, valiant struggle and basically positive personality." Presumably therapist's positive feelings are partly motivated unconsciously by satisfaction with patient's having become independent and well enough to terminate therapy as planned. Patient in turn seems to be pleased that he has successfully fulfilled the therapist-parent's expectations.

Therapeutic Experience of the Patient

In the Interpersonal Relationship

Patient's experience in the interpersonal relationship is fundamentally the same as in Sessions Nos. 65–80. Therapist is consistently warm, supportive, and encouraging, but at the same time continues to indicate that he expects patient to become independent, mature, and to separate himself from the therapy and from therapist. After Session No. 87, when therapist's intention of terminating therapy in the near future becomes evident, there is a partially covert struggle between therapist and patient about the impending termination for a number of sessions because of patient's partially conscious wish not to terminate. Therapist's responses during this struggle are empathically interpretive and supportive, but he remains consistently firm in his intention. Patient finally accepts this as inevitable and endeavors to set the termination date himself as a pride-saving device. Therapist at first opposes this, but later is accepting of patient's assertive wishes.

During the following weeks, patient tries, on the whole successfully, to maintain the independent role, and to deal with—largely by deliberate suppression—his feelings of anxiety, sadness, and anger associated with the separation. He receives recognition and expressions of confidence from therapist about his improvement, his insights, and his capacity to function successfully on his own. This experience is manifestly gratifying, and presumably compensates to some extent for the pain associated with the therapist-parent's desire for him to leave and become independent. Patient's confidence in his ability to function on his own also increases (i.e., his doubts and anxieties are successfully defended against) in response to therapist's attitude. His anxiety about leaving therapy is also diminished by the fact that therapist expresses the wish to see him again in a year and grants him permission to get in touch with therapist earlier if he feels the need for help. Patient ends the therapy with strong positive feelings toward therapist, who in turn feels and explicitly communicates his satisfaction with patient's achievements. Patient is manifestly pleased that he is successfully fulfilling therapist-parent's and his own expectations, and that he is able to give up the therapeutic relationship. Defending against his negative feelings also permits him to retain the image of therapist as the strong, loving, giving parent who still exists in his life, on whom he can depend if necessary and with whom he can continue to identify.

Patient also experiences much narcissistic gratification from therapist when he learns that he is therapist's only patient in the therapeutic project, that therapist spends much extra time thinking about his case, and that patient would ultimately be the subject of a written book.

New or Increased Awareness

During this period Patient had the following new or increased insights:

A. A heightened emotional awareness of the way in which he was using his children to project onto them his conflicts with his brother.

B. A heightened intellectual awareness of his identification with his brother and his fear of breaking loose from his brother; also of how he reconciled accepting the weak position with his brother by shining in brother's reflected glory.

C. Increased intellectual and emotional awareness of his hostility to his sister and its origins; also of his guilt feelings about this, and of the relationship of these feelings to his political views; also of the existence of certain patterns of identification of his wife with his sister.

D. New awareness of his past need to build up his sister-in-law so that she could share the responsibility of his wife with him.

E. Increasing awareness of his hostility to and rejection of his father, and of his wish to repeat the dethroning of the father through therapist. Also of his longing for a good father, due to not having had one in childhood.

F. New awareness that one must learn to live with a certain amount of anxiety.

G. Heightened emotional and intellectual awareness of his separation anxiety and sadness.

H. Heightened intellectual awareness of his tendency to dependently regress at times when he feels stronger and more mature.

Symptomatic or Behavioral Changes

During this period patient either reported or manifested the following symptomatic and behavioral changes:

A. Further reduction of anxiety, tension, and depression, after a transitory increase in these during the working-through of the termination period.

B. Improved relationships and feelings toward his children and his brother.

C. Increased forthrightness and authority in his work relationships (noted by his colleagues and superiors).

D. An increased sense of his own separate identity.

E. Improved sexual relations with his wife.

F. Increased self-confidence, assertiveness, and maturity in his relationship with therapist.

In evaluating the basis for these changes, these are considered important factors:

1. working through and integration of the insights described above (see review of Sessions Nos. 65–80);
2. the corrective emotional experiences due to therapist's manifested and expressed increasing respect for and confidence in patient's strength; also therapist's expectation and encouragement and insistence that he use these strengths and insights;
3. therapist's consistently warm and encouraging behavior throughout this period. The changes and experiences mentioned in the previous section apply also to this section.

At the same time, however, all of the observers and the coordinator raised the question of how much of patient's improvement represented genuine inner growth. Therapist's probing questioning in the final session as to whether patient was "play-acting" evidently reflected some similar doubts on therapist's part. That continued identification with therapist, and incorporation of many of therapist's attitudes and values were taking place in patient throughout this period was evident. There was, in addition, some degree of compliant suppression and repression of his dependent yearnings, separation anxieties, and feelings of anger and sadness during the closing hours as a result of patient's efforts to live up to therapist's expectations. The retention of the image of a strong but loving therapist-parent in the transference is also considered to be an important factor in the changes observed.

Comparison between Observers and Therapist

In this block of sessions the similarities and differences between the therapist's and the team's descriptions are essentially the same as in the previous block. The descriptions of the intellectual-cognitive insights are similar, with the exception of some of the therapist's psychodynamic formulations, which the therapist describes as insights but which the team members do not include in their list of insights.

Both describe the patient's reaction to the imminent termination, the anxiety, sadness, and anger, and the therapist's technique of dealing with it by various interpretations revolving primarily around losing dependency on brother and father figures as patient assumes a separate identity and an independent adult role, and the "pattern of competition-guilt-anxiety-regression." Both the therapist and the team describe the therapist's frequent supportive reassurances about the patient's ability to separate from the therapy successfully. The therapist regards the "insights" and the "working through" of the conflicts as important factors in the patient's being able to terminate.

The team, in contrast, describes a covert struggle between therapist and patient, in which the patient unconsciously attempts to remain in treatment, but yields to the therapist's firm expectation that he terminate. According to the team's description, the patient then attempts to handle his feelings of sadness, anxiety, and anger, and his doubts about ability to function well and lose his symptoms, primarily by the use of suppression and/or repression, as he makes consistent efforts to live up to the therapist's expectations to maintain an adult independent role and master his emotions. As usual, he continues to cooperate with the therapist in the discussions about his inner dynamic patterns. According to the team, he compliantly and more or less successfully suppresses and represses his resentment toward the therapist, and manages to maintain an image of the therapist as a good parent toward whom he feels consciously very warm and grateful.

In some of the summaries the therapist describes some of his conscious attitudes. He mentions his decision to taper off the treatment in order to induce the patient to "face life on his own," and the deliberate use of reassurance to reduce separation anxiety. The therapist also describes his own "positive feelings about the patient as someone who performed well and satisfied the therapist's therapeutic aspirations." The therapist describes his own attitude that the patient must now stop treatment, give up his "natural tendency to continue the dependent patient-therapist relationship and thus protect himself from separation trauma," and must depend on himself and "get his security without swimming with a rope." The therapist also states that he intuitively assumed a more personal relationship with the patient, treating him as a "normal" equal. However, at one point (Session No. 96) the therapist states he is uncertain how to manage termination, and asks himself whether the patient is ready for it.

In general, the therapist's and the team's descriptions of the changes in the patient's behavior and conscious attitudes toward himself and his interpersonal relationships are in agreement. The therapist regards these personality changes as genuine and believes that further consolidation of these changes will take place. He states that he does not expect any serious relapses or sexual impotence, although he describes that in order to deal with his insecure feelings and separation anxiety, the patient tries to persuade himself that he is cured. The team, although agreeing that personality change has occurred, raises a question about how much the patient's improvement represents genuine inner growth.

13

Follow-up Interviews

There have been ten follow-up interviews to this therapy. The first was on 11 December 1959, the last on 19 February 1964.

Due to technical difficulties, not all the material of the ten follow-up interviews was available to the team. Some of these interviews were observed by only one team member. For one or two of the interviews, all that was available was the material derived from the tape and the therapist's report.

The first of the follow-up interviews, on 11 December 1959, took place six months after termination of the therapy at the patient's request, because he did not "feel good." Other interviews were called by the therapist, after he communicated to the patient that he sees patients for a few interviews after the termination of therapy in order to work through some of the unresolved conflicts that, in his experience, come to the fore after therapy is terminated.

All these ten sessions have one characteristic in common—almost always the patient started with the statement that he still has symptoms that concern him. He also realized that he still has certain problems he would like to discuss with the therapist. In addition, he claimed that he now realizes that he feels quite hostile toward the therapist and that he had not dared to express such feelings during the therapy.

The therapist consistently interpreted that the patient was keeping his symptoms alive in order to convince the therapist that he needs more therapy, thus perpetuating a dependency on the therapist. Usually the patient accepted these interpretations. During these sessions the patient was frequently overtly critical and showed some resentment, claiming that the therapist did not take his symptoms and his desire for further therapy seriously. Therapist was consistently accepting of these critical and angry feelings. As usual with him, the patient terminated the sessions feeling better and warmly and kindly toward the therapist. On those occasions that he expressed anger, he seemed relieved and reassured toward the end of the session. The therapist, on his part, has been consistently kind, supportive but firm in his refusal to reopen the case and accept the patient's claim that he still has problems to resolve that required further therapy.

It was the opinion of the observers during these follow-up interviews that a covert struggle was taking place between the patient and the therapist, the patient insisting that he still has symptoms, needed further treatment, and the therapist explicitly opposing continuation of the therapy, because the therapist felt it might have only encouraged a further dependency on the therapist. In these sessions the patient experienced the therapist as a kind but firm parent-surrogate. The patient expressed a good deal of anger toward the therapist and he was able to bring it out much more freely than in the past. He also freely expressed death wishes toward the therapist and he presumably underwent the corrective experience of having these feelings accepted without being rejected by the therapist. During one of these interviews, the patient claimed that the therapist was not much interested in him, but was using him for the purposes of a research project. The therapist was not only pleased by the patient's ability to express hostile feelings toward him but by his ability to stand up to him. The observers who witnessed this interview described that at the end of the session the patient reverted to his compliant or regressive behavior.

During another interview, the patient was able to express a more realistic view of the therapist when he said that the therapist also has "feet of clay" like any other human being, another interesting change in this patient, who had idealized the therapist. In these sessions the patient also relived experiencing the therapist as a substitute parent who was accepting, encouraging, reassuring about the patient's ability to function and about his emotional resources.

In these interviews a definite improvement in the patient was observed. He demonstrated increased recognition of his own worth and heightened self-respect, which he had not shown in the past. Professionally he has made great strides. He has been more recognized and accepted by peers and superiors. His personal life has also improved considerably—his relationships to his wife and children, and his brother, sister, and parents has also been much more mature. His masculine assertiveness has increased and he is more mature than before therapy. His guilt feelings about having surpassed his brother, and his fear of women, derived in the past from fear of his mother, have been appreciably resolved.

The last interview, on 19 February 1964, was held with a member of the team and was not observed. In this session, the patient said he had not been ready to terminate his therapy, but had done so in order to satisfy the expectations of the therapist. This he had become aware of over the years. He realized he had not wanted to disturb the idealized image of the therapist, and he thought the therapist had made a serious mistake in terminating the therapy. He felt the therapist underestimated his discomforts and symptoms, and that the therapist thought he was exaggerating such feelings. He also considered that the relationship with his brother should have been worked through more. He also said that as a result he feels considerable resentment toward the therapist. However, he also said that he was doing considerably better both in his professinal life and in his relations with his family; the relationship to his wife, particularly, was much freer.

This last interview seems to confirm the team's previous impression, that the patient had suppressed and repressed many feelings during the therapy, and that compliance was a major motivation in this patient's behavior during the therapy. However, it also confirms the therapist's opinion and the team's that the patient has made significant changes toward maturity.

14

Conclusions

All of the researchers on this project came to it with a common psychoanalytic bias. All were committed to a belief in the existence of unconscious psychoanalytic processes, including resistance, defense mechanisms, the meaningfulness of dream symbolism, and the importance of transference in the psychotherapeutic process. But perhaps the most important prior conviction that they all shared was the central importance of properly timed and appropriately framed interpretations as the central factor in the therapeutic process.

Although Franz Alexander had already formulated the concept of the "corrective emotional experience" and the belief in its significance in the psychotherapeutic process was shared by most of the observers, nevertheless all of them, Alexander included, considered the interpretive comments of the therapist to be the dominant instrument in his therapeutic armamentarium.

Interpretation was conceived of as something that was given verbally to the patient by the therapist. Its purpose was to develop "insight" in the patient. The insight thus achieved was considered to be the prime factor in the acquisition of therapeutic change. It is true that many analysts had begun to recognize that cognitive insight alone was often not sufficient to bring about a therapeutic change. To be effective it was believed that the insight needed to be linked with an emotional abreaction. Such "emotional insight" was believed to be more uniformly successful in modifying defenses and releasing repressed material from the unconscious, thus opening the path to basic characterological change.

However, the overriding awareness that the observers acquired as they watched and listened to the patient-therapist transactions in the early stages of this research project was how much more complicated the therapeutic process was than they had previously assumed. Rather than being dependent on cognitive insight alone, or on cognitive insight plus emotional abreaction, or for that matter on these combined with corrective emotional experiences, many more variables were involved and could be observed taking place in the patient-therapist transaction. Among these, some of the most important ones could be seen to be taking place nonverbally.

Contrast between Therapist's and Observers' Views

One of the most striking aspects of this study is the contrast between the therapist's and the observers' view of the therapeutic process. The therapist, like most psychiatrists trained in the analytic tradition, tended to place much greater emphasis on, and attribute much greater therapeutic importance to, his cognitive interpretations and the "insights" they were presumably creating in the patient, than did the observers. This is quite understandable. In psychoanalytic therapy the energy and the attention of the therapist is always focused on his efforts to *understand* the psychodynamic roots of the patient's problem and to *verbally communicate* that understanding to the patient.

The observers on the other hand were free to devote more attention to the *transactional* aspects of the therapeutic process, and to *nonverbal* as well as verbal aspects of that process. Thus they were able to observe the effect of the therapist's *personality, value system,* and *style* on the patient; to pick up cues concerning the patient's needs to comply with and please the therapist, and to identify with and model himself after the therapist; to recognize the impact of implicit suggestion and persuasion by the therapist; and to see the way in which the therapist's empathic acceptance of the patient and tolerance of his growing assertiveness constituted corrective emotional experiences for the patient.

Thus it became clear that a good deal takes place in therapy that is not necessarily observed by the therapist and that leads to considerable change in the patient.

The Patient's Initial Set

It was apparent from the outset that the patient came to therapy with certain prior attitudinal sets, preconceptions, and expectations that played a significant role in the nascent patient-therapist relationship. The patient in this study, for example, was an intelligent young man with some prior knowledge of the psychoanalytic frame of reference. He was reasonably verbal and articulate and himself was operating on the assumption and expectation that the psychodynamic insights that the therapist would be giving him would be therapeutically helpful. He was prepared to accept psychotherapy as a "talking process" and adjusted quickly to the basic rule of free association.

A rapid and good working alliance was established that confirmed that a well-motivated patient will adapt to the therapeutic process early in the therapy. The fact that the patient knew that the process was being observed by a team of psychoanalysts was of very little hindrance. After a few initial hesitant steps, the therapy took off and both patient and therapist seemed to work comfortably in this setting.

The therapist, in his professional role as a psychoanalyst, was clearly endowed by the patient as a person with help-giving potential. This is a factor, of course, in almost all psychotherapeutic transactions. But in this instance the therapist was, in addition, a person of considerable reputation and it was apparent to the observers that the patient approached the therapist with considerable deference, awe, compliance, and admiration. He clearly considered it a privilege to be treated by so eminent a person and this, in turn, could not but contribute positively to his expectation of being helped.

Transference and Interpersonal Relationship

As a result of these factors, a positive transference quickly developed in which the patient tended to see the therapist as a strong, idealized father-surrogate, and toward whom he related as a passive, compliant, and submissive son. The patient's unconscious expectation at the beginning of therapy was clearly that if he did what the therapist expected of him—that is, associated freely, brought in dreams, and accepted interpretations, like a good, obedient, and deferential son—the hopes for therapeutic changes would automatically follow. Transference interpretations were not made frequently.

The therapist, however, made it quickly apparent from the early stages of therapy that not only was this an unrealistic expectation but also that he personally rather disliked and looked down on people who appeared weak, submissive, and excessively deferential. The attitudes of the therapist, overtly and covertly communicated to the patient, played a prominent part in the changes that took place in the patient. Compliance with the therapist's wishes, in order to obtain desired gratifications and to avoid painful negative reactions and the feared rejection from the therapist, served as a reinforcement of his already existing values (ego-ideal) regarding independence, self-reliance, and mature masculinity. It appears that the patient lived through a series of experiences with a symbolic parent who, although at times critical and frustrating, was much more consistently helpful and positively interested in his capacities and potentialities for psychological growth and who provided a more masculine model than his actual father had ever done. This is no way implies that cognitive insights, that is, new and increased awareness of his complex inner psychic processes and of the transactions with the significant persons of his life, did not also contribute to the changes.

Catharsis

The opening sessions were characterized by a considerable degree of release of emotional tension as the patient unburdened himself of the various problems that were troubling him. This process is one that was accompanied by a sense of tension relief— an element that is not simply a mechanical process but needs to be understood in the total context of hope and expectation in which it occurred.

Cognitive Interpretation and Confrontations

Very early in the therapeutic process, the therapist began to make various cognitive interpretations to the patient and to confront him with various aspects of his behavior—for example, his excessive dependency, his insecurity, the meaning of his dreams, the nature of his conflicts, and their roots and origins in his early life relationships. The therapist in this instance was quite active, but the differences between his techniques and those of a more formal analysis were more quantitative than qualitative. That is to say, the nature of his interpretations were wholly consistent with the psychoanalytic framework except that in a more classical approach they would have been offered more sparingly and over a longer period of time.

An important factor we learned from this therapy was that significant working through was going on in between therapy sessions. The patient would frequently report at the beginning of sessions the new emotional awareness that would take place after he left the therapist, in the parking lot, or at home, and he would often meaningfully connect such new emotional insight with the work done in preceding sessions. This we consider an important finding, since otherwise we tend to place all the emphasis on what occurs in the therapist's presence. In well-motivated patients what takes place outside the therapy is very significant.

The patient, in turn, showed evidence as he went along of an increasing intellectual understanding (insight) with regard to the sources and nature of his problems. Thus, it became clear that a learning process was going on, with the patient gradually acquiring a cognitive understanding of the basis for his various symptoms and interpersonal difficulties.

Operant Conditioning and the Importance of Nonverbal Cues

Perhaps the most dramatic discovery that the observers made in the course of the project was the importance, frequency, and variety of nonverbal communications that took place between the therapist and the patient during each therapeutic session. The therapist's reactions of approval or disapproval, interest or boredom, and tension or relaxation, revealed in the tone of his voice, in the expressions on his face, and in his bodily posture or movements, were quite apparent to the observers, as were the patient's attitudes and responses. This parameter of communication almost inevitably lies outside of the realm of awareness of both patient and therapist, both of whom are consciously engrossed in the cognitive verbal exchange in which they are engaged. Yet in the course of our months of observation, it became clear that this aspect of the process was a major factor in the therapeutic process. Transference and countertransference reactions occurred in response to these cues, just as much as they did to verbal cues.

Most importantly, however, the therapist's nonverbal responses, no less than his verbal ones, acted as operant condtioning responses, subtly guiding the patient toward the goals of "normal," "mature," or "nonneurotic behavior."

Corrective Emotional Experience

Another fundamental aspect of the therapist's responses, that was both verbal and nonverbal and that contributed another parameter of operant conditioning, was what Alexander has named the "corrective emotional experience." This refers to the therapist's behaving in a different, that is, more objective and constructive, way toward the patient than did the significant authority figures in the patient's past. Alexander considered this aspect of the therapist-patient interaction to be one of the most significant aspects of the psychotherapeutic process, stating his conviction that cognitive insight alone, without this emotional experience, was not enough.

Our observations repeatedly confirmed the correctness of this formulation. For example, whenever the therapist treated the patient as an equal and with respect, one could observe the patient "expanding" with increased self-respect and confidence. Conversely, if the therapist was critical, as he at times seemed to be, the patient appeared visibly crushed. An important turning point in the therapy, however, occurred when the patient, angered by what he regarded as a derogatory remark from the therapist, was able to express his anger openly, not only without receiving retaliation from the therapist, but indeed with obtaining a more accepting and appreciative reaction thereafter from the therapist. It was quite apparent that after this corrective emotional experience, the patient was able to behave more assertively, less deferentially, and with more manifest self-confidence, not only toward the therapist, but also, as he reported, in his extratherapeutic relationships. An important observation we learned from this project was that psychological and physiological responses often find their nonverbal expressions in the therapy and are frequently detected by the patient, either consciously or unconsciously.

Identification

Still another nonverbal manifestation that became apparent in the course of our observations was the subtle and sometimes not so subtle way in which the patient over time began to identify with the therapist. This unconscious process of imitation is, of course, a basic form of social learning (Miller and Dollard 1941) and is facilitated by a positive transference that leads the patient to model himself after the loved and idealized parent-therapist. In this case, the patient could be observed adopting various of the therapist's mannerisms, speech patterns, as well as value orientations. Thus, the therapist, without consciously intending to, became a constructive role model; the patient, by patterning himself after this role model, contributed another facet to the elements leading to therapeutic change.

Suggestion and Persuasion

Another element that our observations brought to light was the degree to which suggestion and persuasion took place in the therapeutic process. Although it might be argued that this particular therapist's style was more active than that employed by many other therapist's, the difference basically is one of degree rather than of substance. The things an analyst chooses to focus on for interpretation or confrontation, no less than those that he chooses to pass over, all reflect value judgments about what he assumes to be "healthy" or "neurotic," "mature" or "immature." To that extent they are not merely cognitive confrontations, but also carry with them an aspect of suggestion and persuasion. These are not less potent because they are often covertly or indirectly, rather than directly, expressed. Indeed, they may be more potent under such circumstances.

Reality Testing

A vital part of the process toward change was the patient's gradual testing of new coping patterns or modes of adaptation in the course of therapy. This "reality testing" is essential to enable the cognitive insights acquired in therapy to be translated into meaningful changes in behavior. It is also part of the process through which the transference interpretations can be applied to other interpersonal relationships and thus generalized.

Although the term *working through* is used in classical psychoanalytic theory to refer to the gradual overcoming of resistances and repressions that stand in the way of the recovery of infantile and childhood memories, our observations in the course of this research would indicate that it is more generally applicable to the process of overcoming resistances to the repetitive testing of reality. The point that Freud made with regard to patients with certain phobias, that a time is reached in analytic therapy when insight alone is not enough and when the patient must be urged to confront his anxieties directly, has more general implications, it seems to us. In a sense, all patients have to deal with anxiety when they are faced with the necessity of trying out new patterns of coping with interpersonal relationships, patterns that they have hitherto been unable to achieve. The insistent pressure from the therapist, sometimes overt, but more usually covert, is for them to begin confronting these anxiety-provoking situations by testing reality. Although this process in dynamic psychotherapy is much less obvious than it is in the behavioral therapies, it bears a direct relationship to the "rehearsal" techniques used by behavioral therapists and to the "practice" that is inherent in learning new techniques in general.

Emotional Support

Consistent and patient emotional support on the part of the therapist is an essential ingredient in enabling the patient to confront reality and test new modes of adaptation in this way. In effect, this emotional support carries the implicit message: "I have confidence in you and in your ability to function at a more mature or adaptive level." Over time the patient is able to introject this repetitive communication and make it part of an improved self-concept.

Appendix
Worksheet for Observers and Therapists

Note: The major purpose of this worksheet is to have a detailed account by trained analytic observers of the events of each hour and, in some instances, their judgment and interpretations concerning those events. The worksheet is designed to allow for both spontaneity and systematic and comparable entries where it is essential to have several judgments on the same event. Also, the worksheet provides for observations which will be made only occasionally. It is not expected that the observers will comment at great length on every point after each hour. However, it is important that the observers indicate that they have "no comment" or that they "did not observe" something; a blank might suggest to the coordinator that the observer just forgot to make an entry and it is then impossible to compare the blank with the statements of other observers or the therapist.

In general, please *describe* what you see, hear, feel, understand. Be as *specific* as you can. If and when you make *inferences*, or put down *hunches*, please say so. Remember, the coordinator wasn't there, the transcript won't always help, and the other observers may see things differently; unless you say so, nobody can tell a hunch from a statement of fact.

171

****

I. OBSERVER AS A PERSON:

Please record here your reactions comparable to those which the therapist records on the keyboard: Physical state including level of energy, feelings toward patient and therapist, periods of more or less attentiveness, insights and theoretical formulations particularly if they influence your observations, and feelings about the project, the coordinators, other observers, etc.

****

II. FREE STYLE, *CHRONOLOGICAL* DYNAMIC ACCOUNT OF THE HOUR: Please describe, in as much detail as you have time for, what happened during this hour.

****

The following sections represent a systematic breakdown of the hour, asking for your comments on points which you may or may not have already touched upon. If you already answered the question and have nothing to add, you may refer to your statement in the free style running account identifying it by an exact reference to the minute(s) for which you made your statement. Please do not just say "see free style account." The coordinators cannot presume to read your mind. By and large, it will be safer to make your comments under each heading.

****

III. EVENTS OF THE HOUR:
1. Central manifest these(s) discussed by the patient:
                              by the therapist:
Here deal with large themes, such as "relationships with men" rather than single topics, such as "brother," "father," "husband," etc.

2. Topics returned to by patient:
   by therapist:
   Specify whether with encouragement or against opposition.
3. Topics evaded by patient:
   by therapist:
   Specify whether by silent avoidance or changing the subject. In the case of the therapist, differentiate between avoidance of a subject which the patient brings up forcefully and silence as part of therapeutic technique.
4. At which points, if any, did you notice a discrepancy between manifest verbal content and non-verbal behavior.
   In the patient:
   In the therapist:
5. Did you notice a meaningful and/or characteristic relationship between content and non-verbal behavior? Specify and describe.
6. What was the period of highest affective intensity? What was it related to? How was it manifested in non-verbal behavior?
7. Style: Describe the manner in which the therapist and the patient put themselves across to you. Include for both the level of energy. Establish a baseline and record deviations.

IV. INTERVENTIONS:
1. Major interpretations and confrontations.
2. Describe the manner in which these are put across to the patient.
3. Describe patient's reactions to them; describe listening behavior during and following interventions.
4. Other important interventions.
5. Same as 2 and 3 for these.

V. THERAPIST AS A PERSON:
1. Therapist's emotions that are revealed by verbal and non-verbal behavior. Try to indicate degree of obviousness and intensity.
2. Therapist's wishes in relationship to the patient.

3. Therapist's reactions of like, dislike, approval, disapproval to something the patient has said or done.
4. General information about the therapist. Include both factual information and values which do not specifically relate to the therapeutic situation.

VI. INTRAPERSONAL PROCESSES:
   1. Main unconscious tendencies or drives in conflict with what?
   2. Free association and resistance.
      a. When did the patient free associate and about what?
      b. What are the defensive maneuvers of the patient during the hour? Against what are they directed?
      Resistance is the manifestation of the patient's unconscious struggle against insight. It is manifested in various defensive mechanisms stimulated by the process of therapy. Some of these defensive devices will be the classical ones, others will be molded by the nature of the therapeutic process.
   3. Transference:
      Transference refers to feelings, ideas, expectations, and behavior of the patient in his relation with the analyst which are not newly created by the objective analytic situation but have their source in early object-relations.
      a. Describe transference manifestations in the patient. Be specific.
      b. Describe transference manifestations in the therapist.
   4. Imitation and identification:
      Imitation is the mirroring of another person's characteristic manner of dress, speech, gesturing, etc. It may or may not be a manifestation of identification.

      Identification is the alteration of the ego following the pattern of the object model.
      a. Describe manifestations of imitation in the patient:
                                              in the therapist (?)
      b. What indications were there for identification with the therapist?

5. Insight and working through:
  a. Manifestations of new intellectual understanding of self, others, external reality, and connections between all these.
  b. New emotional experience.
  c. Repetitions of emotional or intellectual insight.
  d. Repetitions associated with shifts in the elements of a conflict and/or changes in behavior.

VII. SHIFTS AND CHANGES:

Record any change, qualitative or quantitative, that strikes you as noteworthy.

References

American Psychoanalytic Association. 1974. *Conference on Psychoanalytic Education and Research.* Commission VII, Psychoanalytic Research. Position Papers. New York.

Auld, F., Jr., and Dollard, J. 1966. Measurement of motivational variables in psychotherapy. In L. A. Gottschalk and A. H. Auerbach (eds.), *Methods of Research in Psychotherapy*, 85–92 New York: Appleton-Century Crofts.

Bellak, L. 1961. Research in psychoanalysis. *Psychoanalytic Quarterly* 30:519–48.

Bellak, L., and Smith, M. B. 1956. An experimental exploration of psychoanalytic process. *Psychoanalytic Quarterly* 25: 385–414.

Bergin, A. E. 1992. In Freedheim, 1992, 413–22.

Bergin, A. E., and Garfield, S. L. 1971. *Handbook of Psychotherapy and Behavior Change: An Empirical Analysis.* New York: Wiley

Beutler, Larry, and Crago, Marjoire (eds.). 1991. *Psychotherapy Research: An International Review of Programmatic Studies.* American Psychological Assn. Washington, D.C

Beutler, Larry, and Machado, Paulo. 1992. Research in Psychotherapy. In Rozenzweig, Mark R. (ed.), *International Psychological Science.* Washington, DC: American Psychological Assn.

Chance, Erika. 1966. Content analysis of verbalizations about interpersonal experience. In L. A. Gottschalk and A. H. Auerbach (eds.), *Methods of Research in Psychotherapy*, 127–44.

COPER. See American Psychoanalytic Association.

Crits-Cristoph, Paul, Cooper, Andrew, and Luborsky, Lester. 1988. "The accuracy of therapists' interpretations and the outcome of dynamic psychotherapy. *Journal of Consulting and Clinical Psychology* 56: 490–95.

Dahl, H. 1972. A quantitative study of a psychoanalysis. *Psychoanalysis and Contemporary Science* 1: 237–57.

——. 1974. The measurement of meaning in psychoanalysis by computer analysis of verbal concepts. *Journal of the American Psychoanalytic Association* 22: 37–57.

Deutsch, F. 1966. Some principles of correlating verbal and non-verbal communications. Gottschalk and Auerbach 1966, 166–84.

Dewald, P. A. 1972. *The Psychoanalytic Process: A Case Illustration.* New York: Basic Books.

Dittman, A. T., Parloff, M. B., and Boomer, D. S. 1965. Facial and bodily expression: A study of receptivity of emotional cues. *Psychiatry* 28: 239–44.

Dollard, J., and Auld, F., Jr. 1959. *Scoring Human Motives: A Manual.* New Haven: Yale University Press.

Dorpat, T. L., reporter. 1973, April–May. Research on the therapeutic process in psychoanalysis. Panel of the American Psychoanalytic Association, 1972, *Journal of the Psychoanalytic Association* 21: 168–81.

Frank, Jerome D. 1973. *Persuasion and Healing.* 2d ed. Baltimore: Johns Hopkins University Press.

Frank, Jerome. 1992. In Freedheim 1992, 392–96.

Freedheim, Donald K. (ed.). 1992. *History of Psychotherapy: A Century of Change.* Washington, DC: American Psychological Assn.

Garfield, S. L. 1974. What are therapeutic variables in psychotherapy? *Psychotherapy and Psychosomatics* 24: 372–78.

Garfield, S. L., and Bergin, Allen E. (eds.). 1978. *Handbook of Psychotherapy and Behavior Change.* 2d ed. New York: Wiley.

——. 1986. *Handbook of Psychotherapy and Behavior Change.* 3d ed. New York: Wiley.

Gill, Merton M., and Hoffman, Irwin Z. 1982. A method for studying the analysis of aspects of the patient's experience of the relationship in psychoanalysis and psychotherapy. *Journal of the American Psychoanalytic Association* 30: 137–67.

Gottschalk, L. 1978. Content analysis of speech in psychiatric research. *Comprehensive Psychiatry* 19: 387–92.

Gottschalk, L. A., and Auerbach, A. H. (eds.). 1966. *Methods of Research in Psychotherapy.* New York: Appleton-Century-Crofts.

Gottschalk, L. A., and Gleser, G. C. 1969. *Manual of Instructions for Using the Gottschalk-Gleser Content Analysis Scales: Anxiety, Hostility and Social Alienation and Personal Disorganization.* Berkeley: University of California Press.

——. 1969. *The Measurement of Psychological States Through the Content Analysis of Verbal Behavior.* Berkeley: University of California Press.

Gottschalk, L. A., Hausmann, C., and Brown J. S. 1975. A computerized scoring system for use with content analysis scales. *Comprehensive Psychiatry* 16: 77–90.

Gottschalk, L. A., Winget, C. M., Glesser, G. C., and Springer, K. J. 1966. The measurement of emotional changes during a psychiatric interview: A working model toward quantifying the psychoanalytic concept of affect. In Gottschalk and Auerbach 1966, 93–126.

Haggard, E. A., Hiken, Jr., and Isaacs, R. S. 1965. Some effects of recording and filming on psychotherapeutic process. *Psychiatry* 28: 169–91.

Hartly, D. E., and Strupp, H. H., 1983. The therapeutic alliance. In Masling, J. (ed.), *Empirical Studies of Psychoanalytic Theories,* vol. 1, 1–37, Hillsdale, NJ: Analytic Press.

Henry, Wm., and Strupp, H. 1992. In Freedheim 1992, 436–42.

Hoffman, Irwin Z., and Gill, Merton M. 1988. Critical reflections on a coding scheme. *International Journal of Psychoanalysis* 69: 55–64.

Horowitz, L., Sampson, H., Siegelman, E., Wolfson, A., and Weiss, J. 1975. On the identification of warded-off mental contents: An empirical and methodological contribution. *Journal of Abnormal Psychology* 84: 545–58.

Horowitz, Mardi J. 1992. In Freedheim 1992, 442–46.

Howard, K. I., Orlinsky, D. E., and Hill, J. A. 1968. The patient's experience of psychotherapy: Some dimensions and determinants. *Multivariate Behavior Research,* special issue, 55–72.

Howard, K. I., Orlinsky, D. E., Hill, J. A. 1969. The therapist's feelings in the therapeutic process. *Journal of Clinical Psychology* 25: 83–93.

Howard, K. I., Orlinsky, D. E., Trattner, J. H. 1970. Therapist orientation and patient experience in psychotherapy. *Journal of Counseling Psychology* 17: 263–70.

Howard, K. I., Orlinsky, D. E, Perlstein, J. 1976. Contribution of therapist to patient's experiences in psychotherapy: A components of variance model for analyzing process data. *Journal of Consulting and Clinical Psychology* 44: 520–26.

Kachele, Horst. 1988. Clinical and scientific aspects of the Ulm process model of psychoanalysis. *International Journal of Psychoanalysis* 69: 65–73.

Kernberg, Otto. 1972. Summary and conclusions. Menninger Foundation Psychotherapy Research Project. Psychotherapy and psychoanalysis. *Bulletin of the Menninger Clinic* 36 (parts 1 and 2): 181–95.

Kiesler, Donald J. 1973. *The Process of Psychotherapy: Empirical Foundations and Systems of Analysis.* Chicago: Aldine.

Knapp, Peter. 1974. Segmentation and structure in psychoanalysis. *Journal of the American Psychoanalytic Association* 22: 14–36.

Levy, Norman. 1961. An investigation into the nature of psychotherapeutic process: A preliminary report. In J. Masserman (ed.), *Science and Psychoanalysis,* vol. 4, 125–49. New York: Grune and Stratton.

Luborsky, L. 1992. In Freedheim 1992, 396–401.
Luborsky, L., and Auerbach, A. H. 1969. The symptom context method. *Journal of the American Psychoanalytic Association* 17: 69–99.
Luborsky, L., Crabtree, L., Curtis, H., Ruff, G., and Mintz, J. 1975. The concept of "space" of transference for eight psychoanalysts. *British Journal of Medical Psychology* 48: 65–70.
Luborsky, L., Crits-Christoph, P., Mintz, J., and Auerbach, A. 1988. *Who Will Benefit from Psychotherapy?* New York: Basic Books.
Luborsky, L., Graff, H., Pulver, S., and Curtis H. 1973. Clinical-quantitative examination of consensus on the concept of transference. *Archives of General Psychiatry* 29: 69–75.
Luborsky, L., Mintz, J., Auerbach, A., Christoph, P., Bachrach, H., Todd, T., Johnson, M., Cohen, M., and O'Brien, C. P. 1980. Predicting the outcome of psychotherapy: Findings of the Penn Psychotherapy Project. *Archives of General Psychiatry* 37: 471–81.
Luborsky, L., and Spence, D. P. 1971. Quantitative research on psychoanalytic therapy. In A. E. Bergin and S.L. Garfield (eds.), *Handbook of Psychotherapy and Behavior Change*, 408–38. New York: Wiley.
Marmor, J. 1962. Psychoanalytic therapy as an education process. In J. Masserman (ed.), *Science and Psychoanalysis*, vol 5, 286–99. New York: Grune and Stratton.
———. 1964. Psychoanalytic therapy and theories of learning. In J. Masserman (ed.), *Science and Psychoanalysis*, vol 7, 275–79., New York: Grune and Stratton.
———. 1966. The nature of the psychotherapeutic process. In G. Usdin (ed.), *Psychoneurosis and Schizophrenia*, 66–75. New York: J. B. Lippincott.
———. 1975. The nature of the psychotherapeutic process revisited. *Canadian Psychiatric Association Journal* 20, no. 8: 557–65.
Marsden, G. F. 1965. Content analysis studies of therapeutic interviews: 1954–1964. *Psychological Bulletin* 63: 298–321.
———. 1971. Content analysis studies of psychotherapy: 1954–1968. In A. E. Bergin and S. L. Garfield (eds.), *Handbook of Psychotherapy and Behavior Change*, 345–407. New York: Wiley
Matarazzo, J. D. 1972. *The Interview: An Analysis of Speech Behavior.* Chicago: Aldine-Atherton.
Matarazzo, J. D., and Wiens, A. N . 1972. *The Interview: Research on Its Anatomy and Structure.* Chicago: Aldine-Atherton.
Meltzoff, J., and Kornreich, M. 1970. *Research in Psychotherapy.* New York: Atherton Press.
Menninger Foundation Psychotherapy Research Project 1972. Psychotherapy and Psychoanalysis. Final report. *Bulletin of the Menninger Clinic* 36 (Entire issues, parts 1 and 2).
Miller, N. E., and Dollard, J. C. 1941. *Social Learning and Imitation.* New Haven: Yale University Press.

Mintz, J., Auerbach, A. H., Luborsky, L., and Johnson, M. 1973. Patient's, therapist's and observers' views of psychotherapy: A "Rashomon" experience. *British Journal of Medical Psychology* 46: 83–89.

Mintz, J., and Luborsky, L. 1971. Segments vs. whole sessions: Which is the better unit for psychotherapy process research? *Journal of Abnormal Psychology* 78: 180–91.

National Institute of Mental Health. 1975. *Research in the Service of Mental Health: Report of the Research Task Force.* Rockville, Maryland.

Omer, H., and Dar, R. 1992. Changing trends in three decades of psychotherapy research. *Journal of Consulting and Clinical Psychology* 60: 88–93.

Orlinsky, D. E., and Howard, K. I. 1967. The good therapy hour: Experiential correlates of patients and therapists' evaluations of therapy. *Archives of General Psychiatry* 16: 621–32.

Orlinsky, D. E., Howard, K. I., and Hill, J. A. 1975. Conjoint psychotherapeutic experience: Some dimensions and determinants. *Multivariate Behavior Research* 10: 463–77.

Parloff, M. B., Waskow, I. E., and Wolfe, B. E. 1978. *Research on therapist variables in relation to process and outcome.* In Garfield and Bergin 1978, 232–82.

Parloff, M. B. 1992. In Freedheim 1992, 442–49.

Piper, William, Hassan, F. A., Joyce, A. S., and McCallum, M. 1991. Transference interpretations, therapeutic alliance and outcome in short-term individual psychotherapy. *Archives of General Psychiatry* 48: 946–53.

Rice, L. N., and Wagstaff, A. K. 1967. Client voice quality and expressive style as indexes of productive psychotherapy. *Journal of Consulting Psychology* 31: 557–63.

Rogers, C. R., Glendlin, E. T., Kiesler, D. J., and Truax, C. B. (eds.). 1968. *The Therapeutic Relationship and its Impact: A Study of Psychotherapy with Schizophrenics.* Madison, WI: University of Wisconsin Press.

Rozenzweig, Mark. (ed.). 1992. *International Psychological Science,* Washington, DC: American Psychological Assn.

Sampson, H., and Weiss, J. 1986. Testing hypothesis: The approach of the Mount Zion Psychotherapy Research Group. In Greenberg, L., and W. Pinsof (eds.), *The Psychotherapeutic Process: A Research Handbook,* 591– 613. New York: Guilford.

Sampson, H., and Weiss, J. 1992. In Freedheim 1992, 432–36.

Scheflin, A. E. 1966. Natural history method in psychotherapy: Communicational research. In Gottschalk and Auerbach 1966, 263–86.

Schlesinger, H. J. 1974. Problems of doing research on the therapeutic process in psychoanalysis. *Journal of the American Psychoanalytic Association* 22: 3–13.

Sharp, V., and Bellak, L. 1978. Ego function assessment of the psychoanalytic process. *Psychoanalytic Quarterly* 47: 52–72.

Siegman, A. W., and Pope, B. 1972. *Studies in Dyadic Communication.* New York: Pergamon Press.

Simon, Justin, Fink, Geraldine, Gill, Merton, Endicott, Nobel, and Paul, Irving. 1970. Studies in audiorecorded psychoanalysis: II. The effect upon the analyst. *Journal of the American Psychoanalytic Association* 18: 86–101.

Strupp, H. 1960, Some comments on the future of research in psychotherapy. *Behavioral Science* 5: 60–71.

———. 1989, April. Psychotherapy: Can the practioner learn from the researcher? *American Psychologist:* 717–24.

Strupp, H., and Bergin, A. E. 1969. *Research in Individual Psychotherapy.* Washington, DC: National Institute of Mental Health .

Strupp, H., Chassen, J. B., and Ewing, J. A. 1966. Toward the longitudinal study of the psychotherapeutic process. In Gottschalk and Auerbach 1966, 361–400.

Strupp, H., and Howard, K. 1992. *A Brief History of Psychotherapy Reserach.* In Freedheim 1992, 309–34.

Tokar, J. T., and Steffler, V. 1969. A technique for studying an individual and his language: Part 1. Techniques for eliciting patterns of use of individuals' key words. *Psychotherapy: Theory, Research, Practice* 6: 105–8.

Tourney, G., Bloom, V., Lowinger, P. L., Schorer, C., Auld, F., and Grisell, J. 1966. A study of psychotherapeutic process variables in psychoneurotic and schizophrenic patients. *American Journal of Psychotherapy* 20: 112–24.

Truax, C. B., and Mitchell, K. M. 1971. Research on certain therapist interpersonal skills in relation to the process and outcome. In Bergin and Garfield 1971, 299–344.

Van Der Veen, F. 1967. Basic elements in the process of psychotherapy: A research study. *Journal of Consulting Psychology* 31: 295–303.

Wallerstein, R. S. 1986. *Forty-Two Lives in Treatment.* New York: Guilford.

———. 1988. Psychoanalytic science and psychoanalytic research 1986. *Journal of the American Psychoanalytic Association* 36: 3–30.

———. 1989. The Psychotherapy Research Project of the Menninger Foundation. *Journal of Consulting and Clinical Psychology* 57: 195–205.

———. 1992. In Freedheim 1992, 401–7.

Wallerstein, R. S., and Sampson, H. 1971. Issues in research in the psychoanalytic process. *International Journal of Psychoanalysis* 52: 11–50.

Weiss, Joseph, and Sampson, Harold. 1986. *The Psychoanalytic Process.* New York: Garfield.

Weiss, Joseph. 1988. Testing hypotheses about unconscious mental functioning. *International Journal of Psychoanalysis* 69: 87–95.
White, A. M., Fichtenbaum, L., and Dollard, J. 1966. A content measure of changes attributable to psychotherapy. *American Journal of Orthopsychiatry* 36: 41–49.
Ziferstein, J. 1971. Effects of observation of the therapeutic process. *American Journal of Psychiatry* 128: 353–56.

Index